C. S. LEWIS

They Asked for a Paper

PAPERS AND ADDRESSES

1962

GEOFFREY BLES, LONDON

© C. S. LEWIS, 1962

Printed in Great Britain
by Cox & Wyman Ltd Fakenham
and published by
GEOFFREY BLES LTD
52 Doughty Street London WC1

Australia:

33 York Street Sydney
531 Little Collins Street Melbourne
47–53 Castlemaine Street Brisbane
CML Building King William Street Adelaide

New Zealand:
Wyndham Street Auckland

Canada:
10 Dyas Road Don Mills Ontario

South Africa:
P.O. Box 8879 Pallstate House
51 Commissioner Street Johannesburg

Acknowledgements

While much of the material acknowledged below is my own copyright, I would like to thank all those who have allowed me to reprint the papers in this book. *De Descriptione Temporum* was my inaugural lecture from the Chair of Mediaeval and Renaissance Literature at Cambridge and published by the Syndics of the Cambridge University Press in 1954; "The Literary Impact of the Authorised Version" was the Ethel M. Wood lecture delivered before the University of London and published by the Athlone Press of the University of London in 1950; "Hamlet: The Prince or The Poem?" was the 1942 Annual Shakespeare Lecture of the British Academy and was published for the British Academy by Humphrey Milford of the Oxford University Press; "Kipling's World" was a paper addressed to the English Association; "Sir Walter Scott" was a toast proposed to the Edinburgh Sir Walter Scott Club in 1956; "Lilies that Fester" was written for *Twentieth Century* in 1955; "Psychoanalysis and Literary Criticism" was first read to a literary society at Westfield College and then published by the English Association in *Essays and Studies*, Vol. XXVII, 1941; "The Inner Ring" was a Memorial Oration delivered at King's College, University of London, in 1944 and published by Geoffrey Bles; "Is Theology Poetry?" and "On Obstinacy in Belief" were both papers read to the Oxford Socratic Club and published by them in 1944 and 1955 in the *Socratic Digest*; "Transposition" (now slightly augmented) was a sermon preached in Mansfield College, Oxford, and published by Geoffrey Bles; and "The Weight of Glory",

Acknowledgements

which was a sermon given in the Church of St. Mary the Virgin, Oxford, was published first by the S.P.C.K. and then by Geoffrey Bles. I must thank Mrs. George Bambridge, Messrs. Methuen and Macmillan for the use of quotations from Kipling's works.

Since these papers were composed at various times during the last twenty years, passages in them which some readers may find reminiscent of my later work are in fact anticipatory or embryonic. I have allowed myself to be persuaded that such overlaps were not a fatal objection to their republication.

C. S. L.

CAMBRIDGE, 1962

Contents

The origin of each paper is given at its end

1

De Descriptione Temporum

SPEAKING FROM a newly founded Chair, I find myself freed from one embarrassment only to fall into another. I have no great predecessors to overshadow me; on the other hand, I must try (as the theatrical people say) "to create the part". The responsibility is heavy. If I miscarry, the University might come to regret not only my election—an error which, at worst, can be left to the great healer—but even, which matters very much more, the foundation of the Chair itself. That is why I have thought it best to take the bull by the horns and devote this lecture to explaining as clearly as I can the way in which I approach my work; my interpretation of the commission you have given me.

What most attracted me in that commission was the combination "Medieval and Renaissance". I thought that by this formula the University was giving official sanction to a change which has been coming over historical opinion within my own lifetime. It is temperately summed up by Professor Seznec in the words: "As the Middle Ages and the Renaissance come to be better known, the traditional antithesis between them grows less marked."[1] Some scholars might go further than Professor Seznec, but very few, I believe, would now oppose him. If we are sometimes unconscious of the change, that is not because we have not shared it but because it has been gradual and imperceptible. We recognize it most clearly if we are suddenly brought face to face with the old view in its full vigour. A good experiment is to re-read the

[1] J. Seznec, *La Survivance des dieux antiques* (London, 1940), trans. B. F. Sessions (Kingsport, Tennessee, 1953), p. 3.

9

first chapter of J. M. Berdan's *Early Tudor Poetry*.[1] It is still in many ways a useful book; but it is now difficult to read that chapter without a smile. We begin with twenty-nine pages (and they contain several misstatements) of unrelieved gloom about grossness, superstition, and cruelty to children, and on the twenty-ninth comes the sentence, "The first rift in this darkness is the Copernican doctrine"; as if a new hypothesis in astronomy would naturally make a man stop hitting his daughter about the head. No scholar could now write quite like that. But the old picture, done in far cruder colours, has survived among the weaker brethren, if not (let us hope) at Cambridge, yet certainly in that Western darkness from which you have so lately bidden me emerge. Only last summer a young gentleman whom I had the honour of examining described Thomas Wyatt as "the first man who scrambled ashore out of the great, dark surging sea of the Middle Ages".[2] This was interesting because it showed how a stereotyped image can obliterate a man's own experience. Nearly all the medieval texts which the syllabus had required him to study had in reality led him into formal gardens where every passion was subdued to a ceremonial and every problem of conduct was dovetailed into a complex and rigid moral theology.

From the formula "Medieval and Renaissance", then, I inferred that the University was encouraging my own belief that the barrier between those two ages has been greatly exaggerated, if indeed it was not largely a figment of Humanist propaganda. At the very least, I was ready to welcome any increased flexibility in our conception of history. All lines of demarcation between what we call "periods" should be subject to constant revision. Would that we could dispense with them altogether! As a great Cam-

[1] New York, 1920.

[2] A delicious passage in Comparetti, *Vergil in the Middle Ages*, trans. E. F. M. Benecke (London, 1895), p. 241, contrasts the Middle Ages with "more normal periods of history".

bridge historian[1] has said: "Unlike dates, periods are not facts. They are retrospective conceptions that we form about past events, useful to focus discussion, but very often leading historical thought astray." The actual temporal process, as we meet it in our lives (and we meet it, in a strict sense, nowhere else) has no divisions, except perhaps those "blessed barriers between day and day", our sleeps. Change is never complete, and change never ceases. Nothing is ever quite finished with; it may always begin over again. (This is one of the sides of life that Richardson hits off with wearying accuracy.) And nothing is quite new; it was always somehow anticipated or prepared for. A seamless, formless continuity-in-mutability is the mode of our life. But unhappily we cannot as historians dispense with periods. We cannot use for literary history the technique of Mrs. Woolf's *The Waves*. We cannot hold together huge masses of particulars without putting into them some kind of structure. Still less can we arrange a term's work or draw up a lecture list. Thus we are driven back upon periods. All divisions will falsify our material to some extent; the best one can hope is to choose those which will falsify it least. But because we must divide, to reduce the emphasis on any one traditional division must, in the long run, mean an increase of emphasis on some other division. And that is the subject I want to discuss. If we do not put the Great Divide between the Middle Ages and the Renaissance, where should we put it? I ask this question with the full consciousness that, in the reality studied, there is no Great Divide. There is nothing in history that quite corresponds to a coastline or a watershed in geography. If, in spite of this, I still think my question worth asking, that is certainly not because I claim for my answer more than a methodological value, or even much of that. Least of all would I wish it to be any less subject than others to continual attack and speedy revision. But I believe that the discussion is as good a way as any other of

[1] G. M. Trevelyan, *English Social History* (London, 1944), p. 92.

explaining how I look at the work you have given me. When I have finished it, I shall at least have laid the cards on the table and you will know the worst.

The meaning of my title will now have become plain. It is a chapter-heading borrowed from Isidore.[1] In that chapter Isidore is engaged in dividing history, as he knew it, into its periods; or, as he calls them, *aetates*. I shall be doing the same. Assuming that we do not put our great frontier between the Middle Ages and the Renaissance, I shall consider the rival claims of certain other divisions which have been, or might be, made. But, first, a word of warning. I am not, even on the most Lilliputian scale, emulating Professor Toynbee or Spengler. About everything that could be called "the philosophy of history" I am a desperate sceptic. I know nothing of the future, not even whether there will be any future. I don't know whether past history has been necessary or contingent. I don't know whether the human tragi-comedy is now in Act I or Act V; whether our present disorders are those of infancy or of old age. I am merely considering how we should arrange or schematize those facts—ludicrously few in comparison with the totality—which survive to us (often by accident) from the past. I am less like a botanist in a forest than a woman arranging a few cut flowers for the drawing-room. So, in some degree, are the greatest historians. We can't get into the real forest of the past; that is part of what the word *past* means.

The first division that naturally occurs to us is that between Antiquity and the Dark Ages—the fall of the Empire, the barbarian invasions, the christening of Europe. And of course no possible revolution in historical thought will ever make this anything less than a massive and multiple change. Do not imagine that I mean to belittle it. Yet I must observe that three things have happened since, say, Gibbon's time, which make it a shade less catastrophic for us than it was for him.

[1] *Etymologiarum*, ed. W. M. Lindsay, 2 vols. (Oxford, 1911), V, xxxix.

1. The partial loss of ancient learning and its recovery at the Renaissance were for him both unique events. History furnished no rivals to such a death and such a re-birth. But we have lived to see the second death of ancient learning. In our time something which was once the possession of all educated men has shrunk to being the technical accomplishment of a few specialists. If we say that this is not total death, it may be replied that there was no total death in the Dark Ages either. It could even be argued that Latin, surviving as the language of Dark Age culture, and preserving the disciplines of Law and Rhetoric, gave to some parts of the classical heritage a far more living and integral status in the life of those ages than the academic studies of the specialists can claim in our own. As for the area and the *tempo* of the two deaths, if one were looking for a man who could not read Virgil though his father could, he might be found more easily in the twentieth century than in the fifth.

2. To Gibbon the literary change from Virgil to *Beowulf* or the *Hildebrand*, if he had read them, would have seemed greater than it can to us. We can now see quite clearly that these barbarian poems were not really a novelty comparable to, say, *The Waste Land* or Mr. Jones's *Anathemata*. They were rather an unconscious return to the spirit of the earliest classical poetry. The audience of Homer, and the audience of the *Hildebrand*, once they had learned one another's language and metre, would have found one another's poetry perfectly intelligible. Nothing new had come into the world.

3. The christening of Europe seemed to all our ancestors, whether they welcomed it themselves as Christians, or, like Gibbon, deplored it as humanistic unbelievers, a unique, irreversible event. But we have seen the opposite process. Of course the un-christening of Europe in our time is not quite complete; neither was her christening in the Dark Ages. But roughly speaking we may say that whereas all history was for our ancestors divided

13

into two periods, the pre-Christian and the Christian, and two only, for us it falls into three—the pre-Christian, the Christian, and what may reasonably be called the post-Christian. This surely must make a momentous difference. I am not here considering either the christening or the un-christening from a theological point of view. I am considering them simply as cultural changes.[1] When I do that, it appears to me that the second change is even more radical than the first. Christians and Pagans had much more in common with each other than either has with a post-Christian. The gap between those who worship different gods is not so wide as that between those who worship and those who do not. The Pagan and Christian ages alike are ages of what Pausanias would call the δρώμενον,[2] the externalised and enacted idea; the sacrifice, the games, the triumph, the ritual drama, the Mass, the tournament, the masque, the pageant, the epithalamium, and with them ritual and symbolic costumes, *trabea* and laticlave, crown of wild olive, royal crown, coronet, judge's robes, knight's spurs, herald's tabard, coat-armour, priestly vestment, religious habit—for every rank, trade, or occasion its visible sign. But even if we look away from that into the temper of men's minds, I seem to see the same. Surely the gap between Professor Ryle and Thomas Browne is far wider than that between Gregory the Great and Virgil? Surely Seneca and Dr. Johnson are closer together than Burton and Freud?

You see already the lines along which my thought is working; and indeed it is no part of my aim to save a surprise for the end of the lecture. If I have ventured, a little, to modify our view of the transition from "the Antique" to "the Dark", it is only because I believe we have since witnessed a change even more profound.

[1] It is not certain that either process, seen (if we could see it) *sub specie aeternitatis,* would be more important than it appears to the historian of culture The amount of Christian (that is, of penitent and regenerate) life in an age, as distinct from "Christian Civilisation", is not to be judged by mortals.

[2] *De Descriptione Graec.* II, xxxvii.

The next frontier which has been drawn, though not till recently, is that between the Dark and the Middle Ages. We draw it somewhere about the early twelfth century. This frontier clearly cannot compete with its predecessor in the religious field; nor can it boast such drastic redistribution of populations. But it nearly makes up for these deficiencies in other ways. The change from Ancient to Dark had, after all, consisted mainly in losses. Not entirely. The Dark Ages were not so unfruitful in progress as we sometimes think. They saw the triumph of the *codex* or hinged book over the roll or *volumen*—a technical improvement almost as important for the history of learning as the invention of printing. All exact scholarship depends on it. And if—here I speak under correction—they also invented the stirrup, they did something almost as important for the art of war as the inventor of Tanks. But in the main, they were a period of retrogression: worse houses, worse drains, fewer baths, worse roads, less security. (We notice in *Beowulf* that an old sword is expected to be better than a new one.) With the Middle Ages we reach a period of widespread and brilliant improvement. The text of Aristotle is recovered. Its rapid assimilation by Albertus Magnus and Thomas Aquinas opens up a new world of thought. In architecture new solutions of technical problems lead the way to new aesthetic effects. In literature the old alliterative and assonantal metres give place to that rhymed and syllabic verse which was to carry the main burden of European poetry for centuries. At the same time the poets explore a whole new range of sentiment. I am so far from underrating this particular revolution that I have before now been accused of exaggerating it. But "great" and "small" are terms of comparison. I would think this change in literature the greatest if I did not know of a greater. It does not seem to me that the work of the Troubadours and Chrestien and the rest was really as great a novelty as the poetry of the twentieth century. A man bred on the *Chanson de Roland* might have been puzzled by the *Lancelot*. He would have wondered why the author spent so much time on the sentiments and so (comparatively) little on the actions. But he would have known that this was what the author had done. He would, in one important sense, have known what the poem was "about". If he had misunderstood the intention, he would at least have understood the words. That is why I do not think the change from "Dark" to "Middle" can, on the literary side, be judged equal to the change which has taken place in my own lifetime. And of course in religion it does not even begin to compete.

A third possible frontier remains to be considered. We might draw our line somewhere towards the end of the seventeenth century, with the general acceptance of Copernicanism, the dominance of Descartes, and (in England) the foundation of the Royal Society. Indeed, if we were considering the history of thought (in the narrower sense of the word) I believe this is where I would draw my line. But if we are considering the history of our culture in general, it is a different matter. Certainly the sciences then began to advance with a firmer and more rapid tread. To that advance nearly all the later, and (in my mind) vaster, changes can be traced. But the effects were delayed. The sciences long remained like a lion-cub whose gambols delighted its master in private; it had not yet tasted man's blood. All through the eighteenth century the tone of the common mind remained ethical, rhetorical, juristic, rather than scientific, so that Johnson[1] could truly say, "the knowledge of external nature, and the sciences which that knowledge requires or includes, are not the great or the frequent business of the human mind." It is easy to see why. Science was not the business of Man because Man had not yet become the business of science. It dealt chiefly with the inanimate; and it threw off few technological by-products. When Watt makes his engine, when Darwin starts monkeying with the ancestry of Man,

[1] *Life of Milton.*

16

and Freud with his soul, and the economists with all that is his, then indeed the lion will have got out of its cage. Its liberated presence in our midst will become one of the most important factors in everyone's daily life. But not yet; not in the seventeenth century.

It is by these steps that I have come to regard as the greatest of all divisions in the history of the West that which divides the present from, say, the age of Jane Austen and Scott. The dating of such things must of course be rather hazy and indefinite. No one could point to a year or a decade in which the change indisputably began, and it has probably not yet reached its peak. But somewhere between us and the Waverley Novels, somewhere between us and *Persuasion*, the chasm runs. Of course, I had no sooner reached this result than I asked myself whether it might not be an illusion of perspective. The distance between the telegraph post I am touching and the next telegraph post looks longer than the sum of the distances between all the other posts. Could this be an illusion of the same sort? We cannot pace the periods as we could pace the posts. I can only set out the grounds on which, after frequent reconsideration, I have found myself forced to reaffirm my conclusion.

1. I begin with what I regard as the weakest; the change, between Scott's age and ours, in political order. On this count my proposed frontier would have serious rivals. The change is perhaps less than that between Antiquity and the Dark Ages. Yet it is very great; and I think it extends to all nations, those we call democracies as well as dictatorships. If I wished to satirise the present political order I should borrow for it the name which *Punch* invented during the first German War: *Govertisement*. This is a portmanteau word and means "government by advertisement". But my intention is not satiric; I am trying to be objective. The change is this. In all previous ages that I can think of the principal aim of rulers, except at rare and short intervals, was to

keep their subjects quiet, to forestall or extinguish widespread excitement and persuade people to attend quietly to their several occupations. And on the whole their subjects agreed with them. They even prayed (in words that sound curiously old-fashioned) to be able to live "a peaceable life in all godliness and honesty" and "pass their time in rest and quietness". But now the organisation of mass excitement seems to be almost the normal organ of political power. We live in an age of "appeals", "drives", and "campaigns". Our rulers have become like schoolmasters and are always demanding "keenness". And you notice that I am guilty of a slight archaism in calling them "rulers". "Leaders" is the modern word. I have suggested elsewhere that this is a deeply significant change of vocabulary. Our demand upon them has changed no less than theirs on us. For of a ruler one asks justice, incorruption, diligence, perhaps clemency; of a leader, dash, initiative, and (I suppose) what people call "magnetism" or "personality".

On the political side, then, this proposed frontier has respectable, but hardly compulsive, qualifications.

2. In the arts I think it towers above every possible rival. I do not think that any previous age produced work which was, in its own time, as shatteringly and bewilderingly new as that of the Cubists, the Dadaists, the Surrealists, and Picasso has been in ours. And I am quite sure that this is true of the art I love best, that is, of poetry. This question has often been debated with some heat, but the heat was, I think, occasioned by the suspicion (not always ill-grounded) that those who asserted the unprecedented novelty of modern poetry intended thereby to discredit it. But nothing is farther from my purpose than to make any judgement of value, whether favourable or the reverse. And if once we can eliminate that critical issue and concentrate on the historical fact, then I do not see how anyone can doubt that modern poetry is not only a greater novelty than any other "new poetry" but new in a new

way, almost in a new dimension. To say that all new poetry was once as difficult as ours is false; to say that any was is an equivocation. Some earlier poetry was difficult, but not in the same way. Alexandrian poetry was difficult because it presupposed a learned reader; as you became learned you found the answers to the puzzles. Skaldic poetry was unintelligible if you did not know the *kenningar*, but intelligible if you did. And—this is the real point—all Alexandrian men of letters and all skalds would have agreed about the answers. I believe the same to be true of the dark conceits in Donne; there was one correct interpretation of each and Donne could have told it to you. Of course you might misunderstand what Wordsworth was "up to" in *Lyrical Ballads*; but everyone understood what he said. I do not see in any of these the slightest parallel to the state of affairs disclosed by a recent symposium on Mr. Eliot's *Cooking Egg*.[1] Here we find seven adults (two of them Cambridge men) whose lives have been specially devoted to the study of poetry discussing a very short poem which has been before the world for thirty-odd years; and there is not the slightest agreement among them as to what, in any sense of the word, it means. I am not in the least concerned to decide whether this state of affairs is a good thing, or a bad thing.[2] I merely assert that it is a new thing. In the whole history of the West, from Homer—I might almost say from the *Epic of Gilgamesh*—there has been no bend or break in the development of poetry comparable to this. On this score my proposed division has no rival to fear.

3. Thirdly, there is the great religious change which I have had to mention before: the un-christening. Of course there were lots

---

[1] *Essays in Criticism*, III, 3 (July 1953).

[2] In music we have pieces which demand more talent in the performer than in the composer. Why should there not come a period when the art of writing poetry stands lower than the art of reading it? Of course rival readings would then cease to be "right" or "wrong" and become more and less brilliant "performances".

of sceptics in Jane Austen's time and long before, as there are lots of Christians now. But the presumption has changed. In her days some kind and degree of religious belief and practice were the norm : now, though I would gladly believe that both kind and degree have improved, they are the exception. I have already argued that this change surpasses that which Europe underwent at its conversion. It is hard to have patience with those Jeremiahs, in Press or pulpit, who warn us that we are "relapsing into Paganism". It might be rather fun if we were. It would be pleasant to see some future Prime Minister trying to kill a large and lively milk-white bull in Westminster Hall. But we shan't. What lurks behind such idle prophecies, if they are anything but careless language, is the false idea that the historical process allows mere reversal; that Europe can come out of Christianity "by the same door as in she went" and find herself back where she was. It is not what happens. A post-Christian man is not a Pagan; you might as well think that a married woman recovers her virginity by divorce. The post-Christian is cut off from the Christian past and therefore doubly from the Pagan past.

4. Lastly, I play my trump card. Between Jane Austen and us, but not between her and Shakespeare, Chaucer, Alfred, Virgil, Homer, or the Pharaohs, comes the birth of the machines. This lifts us at once into a region of change far above all that we have hitherto considered. For this is parallel to the great changes by which we divide epochs of pre-history. This is on a level with the change from stone to bronze, or from a pastoral to an agricultural economy. It alters Man's place in nature. The theme has been celebrated till we are all sick of it, so I will here say nothing about its economic and social consequences, immeasurable though they are. What concerns us more is its psychological effect. How has it come about that we use the highly emotive word "stagnation", with all its malodorous and malarial overtones, for what other

ages would have called "permanence"? Why does the word "primitive" at once suggest to us clumsiness, inefficiency, barbarity? When our ancestors talked of the primitive church or the primitive purity of our constitution they meant nothing of that sort. (The only pejorative sense which Johnson gives to *Primitive* in his Dictionary is, significantly, "Formal; affectedly solemn; imitating the supposed gravity of old times".) Why does "latest" in advertisements mean "best"? Well, let us admit that these semantic developments owe something to the nineteenth-century belief in spontaneous progress which itself owes something either to Darwin's theorem of biological evolution or to that myth of universal evolutionism which is really so different from it, and earlier. For the two great imaginative expressions of the myth, as distinct from the theorem—Keats's *Hyperion* and Wagner's *Ring* —are pre-Darwinian. Let us give these their due. But I submit that what has imposed this climate of opinion so firmly on the human mind is a new archetypal image. It is the image of old machines being superseded by new and better ones. For in the world of machines the new most often really is better and the primitive really is the clumsy. And this image, potent in all our minds, reigns almost without rival in the minds of the uneducated. For to them, after their marriage and the births of their children, the very milestones of life are technical advances. From the old push-bike to the motor-bike and thence to the little car; from gramophone to radio and from radio to television; from the range to the stove; these are the very stages of their pilgrimage. But whether from this cause or from some other, assuredly that approach to life which has left these footprints on our language is the thing that separates us most sharply from our ancestors and whose absence would strike us as most alien if we could return to their world. Conversely, our assumption that everything is provisional and soon to be superseded, that the attainment of goods we have never yet had, rather than the defence and conservation of those we have already, is the cardinal business of life, would most shock and bewilder them if they could visit ours.

I thus claim for my chosen division of periods that on the first count it comes well up to scratch; on the second and third it arguably surpasses all; and on the fourth it quite clearly surpasses them without any dispute. I conclude that it really is the greatest change in the history of Western Man.

At any rate, this conviction determines my whole approach to my work from this Chair. I am not preparing an excuse in advance lest I should hereafter catch myself lecturing either on the *Epic of Gilgamesh* or on the Waverley Novels. The field "Medieval and Renaissance" is already far too wide for my powers. But you see how to me the appointed area must primarily appear as a specimen of something far larger, something which had already begun when the *Iliad* was composed and was still almost unimpaired when Waterloo was fought. Of course within that immense period there are all sorts of differences. There are lots of convenient differences between the area I am to deal with and other areas; there are important differences within the chosen area. And yet— despite all this—that whole thing, from its Greek or pre-Greek beginnings down to the day before yesterday, seen from the vast distance at which we stand today, reveals a homogeneity that is certainly important and perhaps more important than its interior diversities. That is why I shall be unable to talk to you about my particular region without constantly treating things which neither began with the Middle Ages nor ended with the end of the Renaissance. In that way I shall be forced to present to you a great deal of what can only be described as Old European, or Old Western, Culture. If one were giving a lecture on Warwickshire to an audience of Martians (no offence: Martians may be delightful creatures) one might loyally choose all one's *data* from that county: but much of what you told them would not really be Warwickshire lore but "common tellurian".

The prospect of my becoming, in such halting fashion as I can, the spokesman of Old Western Culture, alarms me. It may alarm you. I will close with one reassurance and one claim.

First, for the reassurance. I do not think you need fear that the study of a dead period, however prolonged and however sympathetic, need prove an indulgence in nostalgia or an enslavement to the past. In the individual life, as the psychologists have taught us, it is not the remembered but the forgotten past that enslaves us. I think the same is true of society. To study the past does indeed liberate us from the present, from the idols of our own market-place. But I think it liberates us from the past too. I think no class of men are less enslaved to the past than historians. The unhistorical are usually, without knowing it, enslaved to a fairly recent past. Dante read Virgil. Certain other medieval authors[1] evolved the legend of Virgil as a great magician. It was the more recent past, the whole quality of mind evolved during a few preceding centuries, which impelled them to do so. Dante was freer; he also knew more of the past. And you will be no freer by coming to misinterpret Old Western Culture as quickly and deeply as those medievals misinterpreted Classical Antiquity; or even as the Romantics misinterpreted the Middle Ages.[2] Such misinterpretation has already begun. To arrest its growth while arrest is still possible, is surely a proper task for a university.

And now for the claim: which sounds arrogant but, I hope, is not really so. I have said that the vast change which separates you from Old Western has been gradual and is not even now complete.

[1] On their identity see Comparetti, *Virgilio nel Medio Evo,* ed. G. Pasquali (Firenze, 1943), p. xxii. I owe this reference to Mr. G. C. Hardie.

[2] As my examples show, such misinterpretations may themselves produce results which have imaginative value. If there had been no Romantic distortion of the Middle Ages, we should have no *Eve of St. Agnes.* There is room both for an appreciation of the imagined past and an awareness of its difference from the real past; but if we want only the former, why come to a university? (The subject deserves much fuller treatment than I can give it here.)

Wide as the chasm is, those who are native to different sides of it can still meet; are meeting in this room. This is quite normal at times of great change. The correspondence of Henry More[1] and Descartes is an amusing example; one would think the two men were writing in different centuries. And here comes the rub. I myself belong far more to that Old Western order than to yours. I am going to claim that this, which in one way is a disqualification for my task, is yet in another a qualification. The disqualification is obvious. You don't want to be lectured on Neanderthal Man by a Neanderthaler, still less on dinosaurs by a dinosaur. And yet, is that the whole story? If a live dinosaur dragged its slow length into the laboratory, would we not all look back as we fled? What a chance to know at last how it really moved and looked and smelled and what noises it made! And if the Neanderthaler could talk, then, though his lecturing technique might leave much to be desired, should we not almost certainly learn from him some things about him which the best modern anthropologist could never have told us? He would tell us without knowing he was telling. One thing I know: I would give a great deal to hear any ancient Athenian, even a stupid one, talking about Greek tragedy. He would know in his bones so much that we seek in vain. At any moment some chance phrase might, unknown to him, show us where modern scholarship had been on the wrong track for years. Ladies and gentlemen, I stand before you somewhat as that Athenian might stand. I read as a native texts that you must read as foreigners. You see why I said that the claim was not really arrogant; who can be proud of speaking fluently his mother tongue or knowing his way about his father's house? It is my settled conviction that in order to read Old Western literature aright you must suspend most of the responses and unlearn most of the habits you have acquired in reading modern literature. And because this is the judgement of a native, I claim that, even if the

[1] *A Collection of several Philosophical Writings* (Cambridge, 1662).

defence of my conviction is weak, the fact of my conviction is a historical *datum* to which you should give full weight. That way, where I fail as a critic, I may yet be useful as a specimen. I would even dare to go further. Speaking not only for myself but for all other Old Western men whom you may meet, I would say, use your specimens while you can. There are not going to be many more dinosaurs.

Inaugural Lecture at Cambridge, 1954

2

The Literary Impact of the
Authorised Version

NO TRANSLATION can preserve the qualities of its original unchanged. On the other hand, except where lyrical poetry is in question, the literary effect of any good translation must be more indebted to the original than to anything else. This is especially true of narrative and of moral instruction. Where the originals are Hebrew it holds in an unusual degree even for lyrical poetry because the parallelism of the form is a translatable quality. There is therefore no possibility of considering the literary impact of the Authorised Version apart from that of the Bible in general. Except in a few passages where the translation is bad, the Authorised Version owes to the original its matter, its images, and its figures. Our aesthetic experience in reading any of the great Old Testament stories or, say, the liberation of St. Peter and the shipwreck of St. Paul, depends only to a small extent on the translator. That is why I hope I may be excused for prefacing what I have to say about the literary fortunes of our English Bible by some remarks on the literary fortunes of the Bible before it became English. What is common, even from the literary point of view, to the originals and all the versions is after all far more important than what is peculiar. And by carrying the story a little farther back we have more chance to be cured of our dangerous though natural assumption that a book which has always been praised has always been read in the same way or valued for the same reasons. Virgil's Homer was very different from Chapman's, Chapman's from Pope's, Pope's from Andrew Lang's, and Andrew Lang's from Mr. Rieu's.

There is a certain sense in which "the Bible as literature" does not exist. It is a collection of books so widely different in period, kind, language, and aesthetic value, that no common criticism can be passed on them. In uniting these heterogeneous texts the Church was not guided by literary principles, and the literary critic might regard their inclusion between the same boards as a theological and historical accident irrelevant to his own branch of study. But when we turn from the originals to any version made by one man, or at least bearing the stamp of one age, a certain appearance of unity creeps in. The Septuagint, the Vulgate, Luther's Bible, or the Authorised Version, can each perhaps be regarded as a book. And in the minds of those who used these translations the impression, if you will the illusion, of unity was increased by the unity of the liturgical context in which they were heard, and also by the doctrine of Inspiration. A belief in strictly verbal inspiration will indeed make all Scripture a book by a single Author. Hence Donne in his Seventy-Ninth Sermon rather comically passes favourable judgement on the style of the Omnipotent, assuring us that "the Holy Ghost is an eloquent author, a vehement and an abundant author, but yet not luxuriant".

The Bible thus considered, for good or ill, as a single book, has been read for almost every purpose more diligently than for literary pleasure. Yet certain *testimonia* to it even on that score can be collected from earlier ages.

The oldest literary appreciation that I know is also the most modern in tone. When Longinus[1] praises the author of Genesis —in his language, "the lawgiver of the Jews"—for sublimity of conception, he seems to express a literary experience very like our own. Genesis is placed beside Homer and in some respects preferred to him. The Bible is being ranked among the classics on

[1] *De Sublim.*, IX.

purely secular grounds. But it would be difficult to cite strict parallels from the ages that follow.

The learned M. de Bruyne in his *Études d'esthétique médiévale* (1946) has collected a mass of evidence about the literary appreciation of Scripture in the Middle Ages. Praise is not lacking; but we certainly find ourselves in an alien world. On the threshold of that period we meet St. Augustine's curious statement that the Bible uses *humillimum genus loquendi*.[1] If this referred to style in the narrower sense, if the Psalms and Prophets seemed to him to use "the lowest language" it would be almost inexplicable. Almost, but not quite; the great, roaring machine of Latin rhetoric can, at times, deafen the human ear to all other literature. But from the context I suppose that St. Augustine is referring to something rather different—to that apparent naïvety or simplicity of the literal sense which offended him until he had been taught that it was merely the outer shell, concealing the *sacramentorum altitudo*.[2] This distinction between the literal or historical sense and the allegorical senses—however these are classified by different doctors—is a fundamental factor in all medieval reading of the Bible. It is no doubt true, and must be insisted on, that no superstructure of allegories was allowed to abrogate the truth of the literal sense. Hugo of St. Victor urges upon his pupils the necessity of mastering the literal sense first. "I think," he writes, "you will never be perfectly subtle in the Allegory unless you are first grounded in the History."[3] Yet this very passage reveals how inevitably the medieval exegesis belittled what we should regard as the actual literary quality of the text. It is clear that Hugo expects his pupils to hurry through the historical sense too quickly and perfunctorily. *Noli contemnere minima haec*[4] he adds,

[1] *Conf.*, VI. v.

[2] *Ibid.*

[3] *Eruditionis Didascalicae*, VI. iii.

[4] *Ibid.*

"Despise not these small things." If you had despised the alphabet you would not now be able to read. An appreciation for which the story of Joseph and his brethren or David and Goliath was merely the alphabet, a necessary preliminary to higher and more delightful studies, may have been keen, but it was very unlike our own. Hence we are not surprised to find him saying that the Scriptures are like a honeycomb. They appear dry on the outside *per simplicitatem sermonis* but are *dulcedine plena* within.[1] Notice how the *simplicitas sermonis* echoes St. Augustine's *humillimum genus loquendi*. Again, the Scripture may be compared to a lyre. The spiritual senses are like the strings: the historical sense is like the wood which does not sound itself but keeps the strings together.[2]

I do not wish in any way to deride the doctrine of multiple senses. Our own age, steeped in the symbolism of dreams and in the allegorical or semi-allegorical work of writers like Kafka and Mr. Rex Warner, will not look down on that doctrine with superiority. We may anticipate a revival of the allegorical sense in Biblical criticism. But it will probably be dangerous, and in the Middle Ages I think it was dangerous, to appreciation of the Historical Books as plain heroic narrative.

St. Thomas Aquinas throws a little more light on the references which we have already met to the "lowness" or "simplicity" of the Bible. He explains why Scripture expresses divine truths not merely through corporeal images but even through images of vile bodies rather than noble.[3] This is done, he says, to liberate the mind from error, to reduce the danger of any confusion between the symbol and the reality. It is an answer worthy of a profound theologian. At the same time, the passage in which it occurs reveals attitudes most hostile to aesthetic appreciation of the sacred

[1] *Ibid.*, IV. i.
[2] *Ibid.*, V. ii.
[3] *Summa Theol. Quaest.* I., Art. IX.

text. It would seem, he says, that Scripture ought not to use metaphors. For what is proper to the lowest kind of learning (*infimae doctrinae*) does not seem suitable to the queen of the sciences. But metaphor is proper to poetry, and poetry is the lowest of all forms of learning—*est infima inter omnes doctrinas*. The answer, so far as it concerns us here, is that poetry and Scripture use metaphor for quite different reasons; poetry for delight, and Scripture *propter necessitatem et utilitatem*.[1] Where a nineteenth-century critic might have said that Scripture was itself the highest poetry, St. Thomas says rather that the highest and the lowest *doctrinae* have, paradoxically, one point in common, but of course for different reasons.

From other medieval writers, notably Ulric of Strasbourg, de Bruyne has collected passages which seem, but perhaps not without illusion, to come nearer to the modern point of view. In general, however, I do not think we shall go too far if we say that medieval appreciation of the Bible is divided from modern by a very wide gulf.

If the medieval approach is alien, that of the Renaissance seems to me sometimes repellent. We reach the age of Ciceronianism, of Humanism, of that deadly classical dignity which so obscured and distorted (along with many other things) the classics themselves. It was an age in which Scaliger could tax Homer with vulgarity and complain that Andromache's lament over Hector smacked of an ill-bred woman—*plebeiam mulierculam*.[2] Where an aesthetic like this prevailed the simple grandeur of *Kings* and *Judges* and the Gospels had little chance of being valued at its true worth. Hence Vida thought that the story of the Passion could be improved by the tinsel of his *Christiad*. In a sense, of course, it is only a literary counterpart to the religious paintings of the time: there, too, vast Vitruvian halls rise as the background to "deep,

[1] *Ibid.*
[2] *Poet.*, V. iii.

abstracted, holy scenes". I leave to others a problem I have failed to solve—why this offends in words so much more than it does in paint—and pursue our immediate subject, by tracing the effect of this movement even on so great a man as Sir Thomas More. In his late treatise *On the Passion* he ventures to put words into the mouth of Our Lord. The thing had been done before. In the *Imitation* it had been so done as to satisfy not only piety but our sense of the Dominical style. But More takes the words in Gethsemane, "This is your hour and the power of darkness", and seems to think they can be strengthened by expansion into the following:

Thys is the shorte whyle that is graunted yee, and the libertie geuen unto darknesse, that nowe ye maye in the night, which till this howre ye coulde neuer be suffered to bryng to passe in the daye, like monstruous rauenyinge fowles, lyke skryche owles and hegges, lyke backes, howlettes, nighte crowes, and byrdes of the hellye lake, goe aboute with your billes, your tallentes, your teeth, and your shyrle shryching outerageouslye, but all in vayne thus in the darke to flee uppon me.[1]

I ought to warn you that I am quoting a translation, that of More's granddaughter. But if anyone looks at the Latin and likes it much better than the English, I shall be surprised. I am not, of course, suggesting for one moment any spiritual flaw. The question is about More's taste. Indeed, the more we reverence him as a man, the more striking the example becomes. Even a man so steeped as he in the spirit of the Dominical utterances could be, by Humanistic rhetoric, so deafened to the majesty of their style.

With the first Protestant translators we get some signs of a changed approach. I would wish to take every precaution against exaggerating it. The history of the English Bible from Tyndale to the Authorised Version should never for long be separated from that European, and by no means exclusively Protestant,

[1] *Works* (London, 1557), p. 1397. D–E.

movement of which it made part. No one can write that history without skipping to and fro across national and religious boundaries at every moment. He will have to go from the Soncino Hebrew Bible (1488) to Reuchlin's Hebrew Grammar (1506), then to Alcala for Cardinal Ximenes' great Polyglot (1514) and north for Erasmus' New Testament in the same year, and then to Luther for the German New Testament in 1522, and pick up Hebrew again with Munster's Grammar in 1525, and see Luther worked over by Zwinglius and others for the Zurich Bible of 1529, and glance at the two French versions of '34 and '35, and by no means neglect the new Latin translations of Pagninus ('28) and Munster ('34–'35). That is the sort of background against which Tyndale, Coverdale, Geneva, and Rheims must be set. For when we come to compare the versions we shall find that only a very small percentage of variants are made for stylistic or even doctrinal reasons. When men depart from their predecessors it is usually because they claim to be better Hebraists or better Grecians. The international advance of philology carries them on, and those who are divided by the bitterest theological hatreds gladly learn from one another. Tyndale accepts corrections from More: Rheims learns from Geneva: phrases travel through Rheims on their way from Geneva to Authorised. Willy-nilly all Christendom collaborates. The English Bible is the English branch of a European tree.

Yet in spite of this there is something new about Tyndale; for good or ill a great simplification of approach. "Scripture," he writes, "speaketh after the most grossest manner. Be diligent therefore that thou be not deceived with curiousness."[1] In the words "grossest manner" we recognise an echo of Augustine's *humillimum genus* and Hugo of St. Victor's *simplicitas sermonis*.[2]

[1] *Parable of the Wicked Mammon,* in *Doctrinal Treatises,* ed. H. Walter (Cambridge, 1848), p. 59.

[2] Burton; Pt. III, Sect. 4, Mem. ii, Subs. 6 (p. 729) "Blasphemous thoughts the scriptures foster, rude, harsh, immethodical."

That rusticity or meanness which we find it so hard to discern in the Bible is still apparent to Tyndale. The novelty is the rejection of the allegorical senses. That rejection he shares with most of the Reformers and even, as regards parts of the Bible, with a Humanistic Papist like Colet; and it is no part of my business to decide whether it marked an advance or a retrogression in theology. What is interesting is not Tyndale's negation of the allegories but his positive attitude towards the literal sense. He loves it for its "grossness". "God is a Spirit," he writes, "and all his words are spiritual. His literal sense is spiritual."[1] That is very characteristic of Tyndale's outlook. For him, just as God's literal sense is spiritual, so all life is religion: cleaning shoes, washing dishes, our humblest natural functions, are all "good works".[2] The life of *religion*, technically so called, wins no "higher room in heaven . . . than a whore of the stews (if she repent)".[3] This would certainly seem to be an attitude more favourable to the literary appreciation of much Scripture than any we have yet encountered. On the other hand Mr. Gavin Bone, whose loss we still deplore at Oxford, has said roundly that Tyndale "hated literature". This is based on his fierce condemnation of medieval romance;[4] a trait which is Humanistic as well as Puritanical. But I do not think he did hate literature. Where he speaks of his own work as a translator he sounds like a man with a sense of style; as when he says that Hebrew and Greek go well into English whereas "thou must seek a compass in the Latin, and yet shall have much work to translate it well-favouredly, so that it hath the same grace and sweetness".[5] More important still is the evidence of his own original works.

I wish I had time to digress on those works. Tyndale's fame as

[1] *Obedience of a Christian Man* (Walter, *op. cit.*, p. 309).
[2] *Parable of the Wicked Mammon* (Walter, *op. cit.*, pp. 100, 102).
[3] *Pathway* (Walter, *op. cit.*, p. 21).
[4] *Obedience* (Walter, *op. cit.*, p. 161).
[5] *Ibid.*, pp. 148, 149.

an English writer has been most unjustly overshadowed both by the greater fame of More and by his own reputation as a translator. He seems to me the best prose writer of his age. He is inferior to More in what may be called the elbow-room of the mind and (of course) in humour. In every other respect he surpasses him; in economy, in lucidity, and above all in rhythmical vitality. He reaches at times a piercing quality which is quite outside More's range: "as a man feeleth God in himself, so is he to his neighbour"[1]—"I am thou thyself, and thou art I myself, and can be no nearer of kin"[2]—"be glad, and laugh from the low bottom of his heart"[3]—"that he might see love, and love again"[4] —"Who taught the eagles to spy out their prey? Even so the children of God spy out their Father".[5] Though it is not strictly relevant, may I be excused, since the fact seems to be insufficiently known, for saying that Tyndale's social ethics are almost identical with those of More?—quite equally medieval and equally opposed to what some call the New Economics. The points on which these two brave and holy men agreed may have been few; but perhaps they were sufficient, if they had been accepted, to have altered the course of our history for the better.

It is not, of course, to be supposed that aesthetic considerations were uppermost in Tyndale's mind when he translated Scripture. The matter was much too serious for that; souls were at stake. The same holds for all the translators. Coverdale was probably the one whose choice of a rendering came nearest to being determined by taste. His defects as well as his qualities led to this. Of all the translators he was the least scholarly. Among men like Erasmus, Tyndale, Munster, or the Jesuits at Rheims he shows

[1] *Wicked Mammon* (Walter, *op. cit.*, p. 58).

[2] *Obedience*, p. 296.

[3] *Pathway*, p. 9.

[4] *Obedience*, p. 136.

[5] *Answer to More*, ed. H. Walter (Cambridge, 1850), p. 490.

like a rowing boat among battleships. This gave him a kind of freedom. Unable to judge between rival interpretations, he may often have been guided, half consciously, to select and combine by taste. Fortunately his taste was admirable.

The history of the Authorised Version has been told so often that I will not attempt to re-tell it, and its beauties praised so lavishly that I will not praise them. Instead, I will proceed at once to its influence as an English book. I shall attempt to define that influence, for I think there has been misunderstanding about it and even a little exaggeration.

Let us begin by distinguishing the various senses in which one book can be said to influence the author of another book.

1. A book may be, in the familiar language of research, a *source*. Lydgate mentions the loves of Mars and Venus. The immediate source might be some book like Boccaccio's *De Genealogia*, the ultimate source is Homer. It would, I think, be quite good English to say that Lydgate was here influenced by Homer. But that is not the most useful way of employing the word in literary history, nor is it generally so employed. If anyone wishes to call a Source an Influence, let him do so; but let him recognise a Source as a very special kind of Influence. Most of us, I expect, would prefer to distinguish Source from Influence altogether. A Source gives us things to write about; an Influence prompts us to write in a certain way. Homer is a Source to Lydgate, but Homer was an Influence on Arnold when he wrote *Sohrab and Rustum*. Firdausi's *Shah Nameh* was Arnold's Source, but not an Influence on that poem. Malory was both a Source and an Influence in Tennyson's *Morte d'Arthur*; elsewhere in the *Idylls* a Source but perhaps hardly an Influence.

If these terms are accepted, we can distinguish the Bible as a Source for English Literature from the Bible as a literary Influence. That it is a Source of immense importance is obvious. For several centuries its persons, scenes, and doctrines were familiar to every

Englishman. They are constantly used for illustration and allusion. But, of course, when the Bible is a Source, there is usually nothing to show whether the Authorised Version is being used or not. The Bible is one Source for Dryden's *Absalom and Achitophel*, but his spelling of Achitophel's name is not derived from the Authorised. We may indeed assume that most authors, and all unlearned authors, after the sixteenth century derived their Biblical knowledge from that version. But this does not seem to be a fact of any importance. The persons and stories would be the same in whatever text they were known. In my view the huge mass of Biblical material in our literature has no place in an account of the Influence of the Authorised Version considered as an English book.

2. It would, I suppose, be possible to say that we are influenced by a book whenever we quote it; but probably no literary historian would wish to use the word *influence* in that way. It would seem to me reasonable to say, for example, that my own habit of immoderate quotation showed the Influence of Hazlitt, but not the Influence of the authors I quote; or that Burton's habit of immoderate quotation might be influenced by Montaigne, not by the authors he quotes. Frequent quotation is itself a literary characteristic; if the authors whom we rifle were not themselves fond of quotation, then, in the very act of quoting, we proclaim our freedom from their influence. It is almost the difference between borrowing a man's clothes for a particular occasion and imitating his style of dress. If English literature is full of Biblical quotation, I would not describe this as the influence of the Authorised Version, any more than I would call Virgilians all those who quote Virgil. I am not saying that to do otherwise would be necessarily an improper use of language: I only think mine useful for the purpose in hand.

3. So far I have been speaking of what may be called flagrant quotation—quotation isolated and proclaimed by typographical devices. But besides this, there is of course the embedded quota-

tion—sentences or phrases from the Authorised Version artfully worked into an author's own language so that an ignorant reader might not recognise them. Our literature is full of this, especially in the nineteenth and early twentieth centuries; in Trollope, Swinburne, and Kipling it becomes a positive nuisance; one contemporary American professor is very seriously infected. To this process the word Influence might much more naturally be applied. Yet even this does not seem to me to be Influence in the deepest sense, and I would prefer not to call it Influence at all. I will try to explain why.

Let us begin by laying side by side with it two other phenomena of the same sort: the ubiquitous embedded quotations from Homer in Plato's prose, or from Shakespeare in English prose. The scraps of Homer slip very artfully in and out of the orchestration of a Platonic period. But of course they are all marked out from their surroundings by their metre and their dialect. No one would maintain that Plato's own style grows out of, or was learned from, Homer's. And indeed the Homeric bits would not be doing their work unless they were felt to be different from the Attic prose that surrounds them. They are used either for solemnity or facetiously—and the facetious is only the solemn stood on its head. The very response they demand depends on our feeling them as aliens. There would be no point in them unless we did. Far from showing that Plato's style has assimilated Homer's, they show the irreducible difference between them. And are not the embedded Shakespearian quotations in English the same? Of course, not every hack who speaks of a man more sinned against than sinning, or a consummation devoutly to be wished, knows that he is quoting Shakespeare. He may think (significantly) that he is quoting the Bible. He may even think he is using a proverb. But he knows quite well, and he expects his readers to know, that he is borrowing from somewhere. He counts on recognition. He is decorating his style. He wants the phrase to stand out from his own composition as gold lace stands out from a coat. The whole pleasure, such as it is, depends on the fact that the embedded quotation is different—in other words that his own style is not influenced by Shakespeare.

I believe that our embedded quotations from the Authorised Version are nearly always in exactly this position. They are nearly always either solemn or facetious. Only because the surrounding prose is different—in other words, only in so far as our English is not influenced by the Authorised Version—do they achieve the effect the authors intended.

4. Here at last we reach what I would describe as Influence in the full and strict sense—the influence of the Authorised Version on vocabulary. I do not think we are being (in this sense) influenced by Shakespeare when we speak of a consummation devoutly to be wished. But I do think we are influenced by him (though the phonetic history is complicated) whenever we use *weird* as an adjective. We do so with no sense of quotation: the word has been really assimilated, has gone into the blood-stream of our language. In the same way we are being influenced by Van Helmont (and perhaps by Paracelsus) whenever we use the word *gas*. In the same way we are being influenced by the Authorised Version and its predecessors whenever we use the words *beautiful, long-suffering, peacemaker* or *scapegoat*. Tyndale is our ultimate creditor for all these. But even here I must plead for a distinction. Henry Bradley rightly mentioned *damsel, raiment, travail,* and *quick* in the sense "alive", as words saved by the Authorised Version for archaic and poetical use. But only for such use. They are not in the blood-stream. As for *loving-kindness* and *tender mercies,* they are so generally confined either to religious contexts or to mockery (which for our special purpose tells the same tale) that I almost classify them as very short embedded quotations.

5. Finally, we come to literary influence in the fullest sense, the sense it bears when we say that *Paradise Lost* is influenced by

Homer and Virgil, or nineteenth-century journalism by Macaulay, or modern English poetry by Mr. Eliot. You will perhaps remember that I have defined Influence, in this sense, as that which prompts a man to write in a certain way. But even within this definition further distinctions break out. The influence may show itself in architectonics. That is the most obvious, though by no means the only, manner in which Virgil influences Milton. The whole plan of his epic is Virgilian. Very few English writers have undergone an influence of that sort from any book of the Bible. Tupper's *Proverbial Philosophy* and the *Book of Mormon* are perhaps instances. Some would add Blake's *Prophetic Books*. Again, Influence may show itself in the use of language—in the rhythm, the imagery, or (using that word in its narrowest sense) the style.

The influence of the rhythms of the Authorised Version seems to me to be very hard to detect. Its rhythms are in fact extremely various, and some of them are unavoidable in the English language. I am not at all sure that a resemblance in rhythm, unless supported by some other resemblance, is usually recognisable. If I say "At the regatta Madge avoided the river and the crowd" would this, without warning, remind you of "In the beginning God created the heaven and the earth"? Even if it did, is the common rhythm, thus separated from community of thought and temper, a matter of any importance? I believe that wherever an English writer seems to us to recall the scriptural rhythms, he is always recalling other associations as well. The influence of rhythm, isolated from imagery and style, is perhaps an abstraction.

In imagery I suppose the influence to be very great, though I must frankly confess that I have not been able to invent a method of checking it. If English writers in elevated contexts tend to speak of corn and wine rather than of beef and beer and butter, of chariots rather than chargers, of rain rather than sunshine as a characteristic blessing, of sheep more often than cows and of the sword more often than either the pike or the gun, of bread rather than mutton or potatoes is their lofty synonym for food, if stone is more poetical than brick, trumpets than bugles and purple and fine linen loftier than satin and velvet, I suspect that this is due to the Bible, but I have no rigorous proof. Nor, in this sphere, would it be easy to distinguish the Biblical influence from that generally Mediterranean and ancient influence which comes from the classics as well as the Bible. But I believe the Biblical influence is here very great.

But in our style, in the actual build of our sentences, I think the influence has possibly been less than we suppose. The perfect example of an influence in this field is that exercised on our prose by Dryden and his contemporaries (Tillotson and the like). You remember that he went all through the *Essay on Dramatic Poesy* and altered every sentence that ended with a preposition. This is, I say, a perfect example of Influence. No one can pretend that this curious taboo was inherent in the genius of the language and would have developed even without the action of Dryden and his fellow Gallicists. On the contrary, it is so alien from the language that it has never penetrated into the conversation of even the worst prigs, and serves no purpose but to increase those little bunches of unemphatic monosyllables that English was already prone to. On the other hand, it has so established itself in our formal style that thousands obey it unconsciously. It is, very precisely, a thing that prompts us to write in a certain way : even I, who detest it for a frenchified schoolroom superstition, often feel it plucking at my elbow. I doubt whether the Authorised Version has achieved any comparable dominance over our style. Indeed, what astonishes me here is the failure of some of its most familiar terms to get into our language at all. *It came to pass, answered and said, lo*—have these ever been used by any English writer without full consciousness that he was quoting? If we look into those authors who are usually said to be influenced by the style of the Authorised Version, we shall find that such influence is indeed present but that it is hardly dominant. I will consider Ruskin and Bunyan.

In Ruskin embedded quotation and imagery from the Bible are made great use of, but Homer and Spenser are used not very much less, Dante not infrequently. And all these are used consciously. What Ruskin tells us in *Praeterita*[1] about the formation of his own style is relevant:

Had it not been for constant reading of the Bible, I might probably have taken Johnson for my model of English. To a useful extent I have always done so; in these first essays, partly because I could not help it, partly of set, and well set, purpose ... The turns and returns of reiterated *Rambler* and iterated *Idler* fastened themselves in my ears and mind: nor was it possible for me, till long afterwards, to quit myself of Johnsonian symmetry, in sentences intended either with swordsman's or paviour's blow, to cleave an enemy's crest or drive down the oaken pile of a principle.

In his mature style—in this very passage—I think we can recognise the Johnsonian element: I cannot recognise the Biblical. Elsewhere, though I do not deny its presence—and especially in the images—it is one of many resources. I think *resources* is the best word. It is, so to speak, one of the colours in his paint box, used at his own discretion. He has many others. And what makes the total effect, for me, so very unlike the Authorised Version, is the periodic structure of Ruskin's prose. Already in the passage quoted, which is familiar and epistolary compared with the high passages in *Modern Painters* or *The Stones of Venice,* you will have noticed the transition *nor was it possible.* That is learned from classical Latin. And so, in the long run, is the Ruskinian period as a whole. A structure descending from Cicero through the prose of Hooker, Milton, and Taylor, and then enriched with romantic colouring for which Homer and the Bible are laid under contribution—that seems to me the formula for Ruskin's style. If you

[1] XII.

41

could take away what comes from the Bible it would be impaired. It would hardly, I think, be crippled. It would certainly not be annihilated. This is real influence, but limited influence. The influence of Italian epic on Spenser would be a good contrast. If you took away from the *Faerie Queen* everything that is learned from Ariosto and Boiardo, what would be left would be either nothing or a radically different poem. This is quite consistent with the view that Spenser has added something of his own and even transmuted his originals. The alchemist may turn silver into gold: but he has to have the silver.

Bunyan, at first sight, will strike most of us as far more Biblical than Ruskin. But this impression is partly due to the fact that both are to us rather archaic and rather simple in syntax. To that extent any unlearned author of Bunyan's time would be bound to remind us of the Bible whether he had ever read it or not. We must discount that accidental similarity and look deeper. I take an example at random:

So *Mistrust* and *Timorous* ran down the hill, and Christian went on his way. But thinking again of what he heard from the men, he felt in his bosom for his Roll, that he might read therein and be comforted; but he felt, and found it not. Then was Christian in great distress, and knew not what to do, for he wanted that which used to relieve him, and that which should have been his pass into the Celestial City. Hence therefore he began to be much perplexed and knew not what to do. At last he bethought that he had slept in the Arbour.

The question is not how much of this might occur in the Authorised Version, but how much might be expected to occur in Bunyan if he had not read it. Much of it, of course, is quite unlike the Bible: phrases like *Then was Christian in great distress, he wanted that which used to relieve him, Here therefore he began to be much perplexed.* There remain *he went on his way, he felt and found it not,* and the use of *so* to introduce a new step in a narrative.

These are in the manner of the Authorised Version—though this use of *so* is not very common there and is far commoner in Malory. But I do not feel at all certain that Bunyan is deriving them from his Bible. And if we look through his work we shall find that his best and most characteristic sentences often have a very un-scriptural ring:

But the man, not at all discouraged, fell to cutting and hacking most fiercely.

So I looked up in my Dream and saw the clouds rack at an unusual rate, upon which I heard a great sound of a Trumpet . . .

Why, he objected against Religion itself; he said it was a pitiful, low, sneaking business for a man to mind Religion.

Some also have wished that the next way to their Father's house were here, that they might be troubled no more with either Hills or Mountains to go over: but the way is the way, and there's an end.

At last he came in, and I will say that for my Lord, he carried it wonderful lovingly to him. There were but a few good bits at the Table but some of it was laid upon his Trencher.

Such passages seem to me the essential Bunyan. His prose comes to him not from the Authorised Version but from the fireside, the shop, and the lane. He is as native as Malory or Defoe. The Scriptural images themselves take on a new homeliness in these surroundings: "She said she was sent for to go to her Husband: and then she up and told us how she had seen him in a dream, dwelling in a curious place among Immortals, wearing a Crown playing upon a Harp." The Crown and Harp come no doubt, from the Apocalypse, but the rest of the sentence comes from Bedfordshire and in their village setting they are somehow trans-formed. Just so his Delectable Mountains are Bedfordshire hills magnified, green to the top. Without the Bible he would not have written the *Pilgrim's Progress* at all, for his mind would have been utterly different; but its style might have been much the same without the Authorised Version.

If I am right in thinking that the Authorised Version as a strictly literary influence has mattered less than we have often supposed, it may be asked how I account for the fact. I think there are two explanations.

In the first place, we must not assume that it always gave so much literary pleasure as it did in the nineteenth century. Thanks to Professor Sutherland, most of us now know about the egregious Edward Harwood who in 1768 published his *Liberal Translation of the New Testament: Being an Attempt to translate the Sacred Writings with the same Freedom, Spirit and Elegance With which other English Translations of the Greek Classics have lately been executed.* Harwood wrote to substitute "the elegance of modern English" for "the bald and barbarous language of the old vulgar version". And no doubt Harwood was, by our standards, an ass. But can he have been the only one of his kind? Or does he voice a widely spread feeling which only reverence concealed? "Bald and barbarous", lacking in elegance . . . we have heard something not quite unlike this before: "the most grossest manner," *simplicitas sermonis, humillimum genus loquendi.* It is not a charge anyone would be likely to bring against the Authorised Version or its originals today. Those who dislike Scripture are now more likely to call its style florid or inflated; those who like it would praise it for sublimity. When and how did this change occur?

The answer, I suggest, is that the modern approach, or what was till lately the modern approach, to the Bible is deeply influenced by the Romantic Movement; by which I here mean not the Lake Poets but that taste for the primitive and the passionate which can be seen growing through nearly the whole of the eighteenth century. The men who were engaged in exhuming the ballads, the Elder Edda, the Sagas, the *Nibelungenlied* and the *Kalevala,* the forgers of *Otranto* and *Ossian,* those who dreamed of

44

bards and druids, must have heard the Bible with new ears. The primitive simplicity of a world in which kings could be shepherds, the abrupt and mysterious manner of the prophets, the violent passions of bronze-age fighting men, the background of tents and flocks and desert and mountain, the village homeliness of Our Lord's parables and metaphors, now first, I suspect, became a positive literary asset. The "vile bodies" which St. Thomas had to explain were no longer felt to be vile. Something of the same sort was happening to Homer. Scaliger had found him low. Chapman had reverenced him for his hidden wisdom. With Pope's preface we reach a different attitude. "I would not be as delicate," he says, "as those modern critics who are shocked at the servile offices and mean employments in which we sometimes see the heroes of Homer engaged. There is a pleasure in taking a view of that simplicity, in opposition to the luxury of succeeding ages; in beholding monarchs without their guards, princes tending their flocks, and princesses drawing water from the springs." He significantly adds that he has admitted into his version "several of those general phrases and manners of expression which have attained a veneration even in our language from being used in the Old Testament".

I suggest, then, that until the Romantic taste existed the Authorised Version was not such an attractive model as we might suppose. That would be one cause limiting its influence. The second cause was, I believe, its familiarity.

This may sound paradoxical, but it is seriously meant. For three centuries the Bible was so well known that hardly any word or phrase, except those which it shared with all English books whatever, could be borrowed without recognition. If you echoed the Bible everyone knew that you were echoing the Bible. And certain associations were called up in every reader's mind; sacred associations. All your readers had heard it read, as a ritual or almost ritual act, at home, at school, and in church. This did not mean that reverence prevented all Biblical echoes. It did mean that they would only be used either with conscious reverence or with conscious irreverence, either religiously or facetiously. There could be a pious use and a profane use : but there could be no ordinary use. Nearly all that was Biblical was recognisably Biblical, and all that was recognised was *sacer*, numinous; whether on that account to be respected or on that account to be flouted makes very little difference. Mark what Boswell says under Sat. April 3d. 1773 :

He [sc. Dr. Johnson] disapproved of introducing scripture phrases into secular discourses. This seemed to me a question of some difficulty. A scripture expression may be used like a highly classical phrase to produce an instantaneous strong impression.

"Like a highly classical phrase"—that is the point; and producing a strong impression. It is difficult to conceive conditions less favourable to that unobtrusive process of infiltration by which a profound literary influence usually operates. An influence which cannot evade our consciousness will not go very deep.

It may be asked whether now, when only a minority of Englishmen regard the Bible as a sacred book, we may anticipate an increase of its literary influence. I think we might if it continued to be widely read. But this is not very likely. Our age has, indeed, coined the expression "the Bible as literature". It is very generally implied that those who have rejected its theological pretensions nevertheless continue to enjoy it as a treasure house of English prose. It may be so. There may be people who, not having been forced upon familiarity with it by believing parents, have yet been drawn to it by its literary charms and remained as constant readers. But I never happen to meet them. Perhaps it is because I live in the provinces. But I cannot help suspecting, if I may make an Irish bull, that those who read the Bible as literature do not read the Bible.

It would be strange if they did. If I am right in thinking that the Bible, apart from its sacred character, appeals most easily to a Romantic taste, we must expect to find it neglected and even disliked in our own age. The Counter-Romantic movement is indeed so violent that those of us who do not share it almost wonder if there is not something pathological in the violence. The hatred of Romanticism has reached that stage at which it can see no differences of kind between the things hated. I read the other day an essay in which the author dismissed Chesterton's *Ballad of the White Horse* on the ground that "Morris manages these things better than Chesterton ever did; and nobody wants to preserve William Morris". I can understand, even if I deplore, the taste that does not want to preserve William Morris. What staggers me is the implication that Chesterton and Morris wrote the same sort of poetry. It is as if a man said "Holbein does all these things better than Titian". I can only conclude that the author's revulsion from Romantic poetry has reached a degree of violence at which the difference between the cool water-colour effects of Morris, his northern bareness, and his monotonous plashing melody cannot be distinguished from all the gold and scarlet and all the orgiastic drum-beats of Chesterton. Phobias make strange bedfellows. Perhaps to those who cannot endure the presence of a cat, the huge, square-headed tabby Tom and the little smoke-faced goblin from Siam are all one. But clearly in an age so anti-Romantic as this, all those qualities which once helped the Bible as literature will work against it. David weeping over Absalom, Moses at the Burning Bush, Elijah on Carmel, the Horror of Great Darkness, the Maniac among the Tombs—what have these passages to say to an unbeliever unless he is a Romantic or to a Counter-Romantic unless he is a believer?

What I am saying involves the view that an approach to the Bible which seemed to many of us in our youth to be simply human, was in reality the product of a particular period in the history of taste. I hope you will find this the more credible because of our brief glances at the Bible's earlier history. The Medieval taste for which the literal sense was merely the dry crust of the honeycomb concealing the golden sweetness of the allegory, and the Humanistic taste which felt that the simplicity of Scripture would be improved by rhetoric, may each have seemed, in its own day, natural and eternal. Against that background we can see in proper perspective the eighteenth- and nineteenth-century taste. No doubt we may conclude that the Counter-Romantic taste of the twentieth will also prove ephemeral; indeed, whatever the hidden fuel may be, it can hardly blaze in its present fury for very long. It will be succeeded by other attitudes which we cannot predict.

Inevitably we ask whether any of these is likely to be favourable to a literary appreciation of the Bible. Stripped (for most readers) of its divine authority, stripped of its allegorical senses, denied a romantic welcome for its historical sense, will it none the less return on the wave of some new fashion to literary pre-eminence and be read? And of course we do not know. I offer my guess. I think it very unlikely that the Bible will return as a book unless it returns as a sacred book. Longinus could enjoy it without being a Christian. But then Longinus came as near to being a Romantic as a Greek could, and his view of the world and man was in its own way a religious one.[1] It would be rash to expect many more of his kind. Unless the religious claims of the Bible are again acknowledged, its literary claims will, I think, be given only "mouth honour" and that decreasingly. For it is, through and through, a sacred book. Most of its component parts were written, and all of them were brought together, for a purely religious purpose. It contains good literature and bad literature. But even the good literature is so written that we can seldom disregard its sacred character. It is easy enough to read Homer while suspend-

[1] v. cap. XXXIV.

ing our disbelief in the Greek pantheon; but then the *Iliad* was not composed chiefly, if at all, to enforce obedience to Zeus and Athene and Poseidon. The Greek tragedians are more religious than Homer, but even there we have only religious speculation or at least the poet's personal religious ideas; not dogma. That is why we can join in. Neither Aeschylus nor even Virgil tacitly prefaces his poetry with the formula "Thus say the gods". But in most parts of the Bible everything is implicitly or explicitly introduced with "Thus saith the Lord". It is, if you like to put it that way, not merely a sacred book but a book so remorselessly and continuously sacred that it does not invite, it excludes or repels, the merely aesthetic approach. You can read it as literature only by a *tour de force*. You are cutting the wood against the grain, using the tool for a purpose it was not intended to serve. It demands incessantly to be taken on its own terms: it will not continue to give literary delight very long except to those who go to it for something quite different. I predict that it will in the future be read as it always has been read, almost exclusively by Christians.

If many critics, especially older critics, speak of it differently today, I suggest that they may be influenced by amiable but unliterary motives. A sacred book rejected is like a king dethroned. Towards either of them there arises in well-disposed minds a chivalrous compunction. One would like to concede everything except the thing really at issue. Having supported the deposition, one would wish to make it clear that one had no personal malice. Just because you cannot countenance a restoration, you are anxious to speak kindly of the old gentleman in his personal capacity—to praise his fund of anecdote or his collection of butterflies. I cannot help thinking that when a critic old enough to remember the Bible in its power prophesies for it a great future as literature, he is often unconsciously swayed by similar motives. But such courtesies will not preserve it. Neither the Bible nor those who still read it as believers invite them; and the generation which is now growing up will disregard them. For the Bible, whether in the Authorised or in any other version, I foresee only two possibilities; either to return as a sacred book or to follow the classics, if not quite into oblivion yet into the ghost-life of the museum and the specialist's study. Except, of course, among the believing minority who read it to be instructed and get literary enjoyment as a by-product.

The Ethel M. Wood Lecture, the University of London, 1950

3

Hamlet: The Prince or The Poem?

A CRITIC who makes no claim to be a true Shakespearian scholar and who has been honoured by an invitation to speak about Shakespeare to such an audience as this, feels rather like a child brought in at dessert to recite his piece before the grown-ups. I have a temptation to furbish up all my meagre Shakespearian scholarship and to plunge into some textual or chronological problem in the hope of seeming, for this one hour, more of an expert than I am. But it really wouldn't do. I should not deceive you: I should not even deceive myself. I have therefore decided to bestow all my childishness upon you.

And first, a reassurance. I am not going to advance a new interpretation of the character of Hamlet. Where great critics have failed I could not hope to succeed; it is rather my ambition (a more moderate one, I trust) to understand their failure. The problem I want to consider today arises in fact not directly out of the Prince's character nor even directly out of the play, but out of the state of criticism about the play.

To give anything like a full history of this criticism would be beyond my powers and beyond the scope of a lecture; but, for my present purpose, I think we can very roughly divide it into three main schools or tendencies. The first is that which maintains simply that the actions of Hamlet have not been given adequate motives and that the play is so far bad. Hanmer is perhaps the earliest exponent of this view. According to him Hamlet is made to procrastinate because "had he gone naturally to work, there would have been an end to our play". But then, as Hanmer points out, Shakespeare ought to have "contrived some good reason" for the procrastination. Johnson, while praising the tragedy for its "variety", substantially agrees with Hanmer: "of the feigned madness of Hamlet there appears no adequate cause". Rümelin thinks that the "wisdom" which Shakespeare has chosen to hide under "the wild utterances of insanity" is a "foreign and disturbing element" as a result of which the piece "presents the greatest discrepancies". In our own time Mr. Eliot has taken the same view: *Hamlet* is rather like a film on which two photographs have been taken—an unhappy superposition of Shakespeare's work "upon much cruder material". The play "is most certainly an artistic failure". If this school of critics is right, we shall be wasting our time in attempting to understand why Hamlet delayed. The second school, on the other hand, thinks that he did not delay at all but went to work as quickly as the circumstances permitted. This was Ritson's view. The word of a ghost, at second hand, "would scarcely in the eye of the people have justified his killing their king". That is why he "counterfeits madness and . . . puts the usurper's guilt to the test of a play". Klein, after a very fierce attack on critics who want to make the Prince of Denmark "a German half-professor, all tongue and no hand", comes to the same conclusion. So does Werder, and so does MacDonald; and the position has been brilliantly defended in modern times. In the third school or group I include all those critics who admit that Hamlet procrastinates and who explain the procrastination by his psychology. Within this general agreement there are, no doubt, very great diversities. Some critics, such as Hallam, Sievers, Raleigh, and Clutton Brock, trace the weakness to the shock inflicted upon Hamlet by the events which precede, and immediately follow, the opening of the play; others regard it as a more permanent condition; some extend it to actual insanity, others reduce it to an almost amiable flaw in a noble nature. This third group, which boasts the names of Richardson, Goethe, Coleridge,

Schlegel, and Hazlitt, can still, I take it, claim to represent the central and, as it were, orthodox line of *Hamlet* criticism.

Such is the state of affairs; and we are all so accustomed to it that we are inclined to ignore its oddity. In order to remove the veil of familiarity I am going to ask you to make the imaginative effort of looking at this mass of criticism as if you had no independent knowledge of the thing criticized. Let us suppose that a picture which you have not seen is being talked about. The first thing you gather from the vast majority of the speakers—and a majority which includes the best art critics—is that this picture is undoubtedly a very great work. The next thing you discover is that hardly any two people in the room agree as to what it is a picture of. Most of them find something curious about the pose, and perhaps even the anatomy, of the central figure. One explains it by saying that it is a picture of the raising of Lazarus, and that the painter has cleverly managed to represent the uncertain gait of a body just recovering from the stiffness of death. Another, taking the central figure to be Bacchus returning from the conquest of India, says that it reels because it is drunk. A third, to whom it is self-evident that he has seen a picture of the death of Nelson, asks with some temper whether you expect a man to look quite normal just after he has been mortally wounded. A fourth maintains that such crudely representational canons of criticism will never penetrate so profound a work, and that the peculiarities of the central figure really reflect the content of the painter's subconsciousness. Hardly have you had time to digest these opinions when you run into another group of critics who denounce as a pseudo-problem what the first group has been discussing. According to this second group there is nothing odd about the central figure. A more natural and self-explanatory pose they never saw and they cannot imagine what all the pother is about. At long last you discover—isolated in a corner of the room, somewhat frowned upon by the rest of the company, and including few

53

reputable *connoisseurs* in its ranks—a little knot of men who are whispering that the picture is a villainous daub and that the mystery of the central figure merely results from the fact that it is out of drawing.

Now if all this had really happened to any one of us, I believe that our first reaction would be to accept, at least provisionally, the third view. Certainly I think we should consider it much more seriously than we usually consider those critics who solve the whole *Hamlet* problem by calling *Hamlet* a bad play. At the very least we should at once perceive that they have a very strong case against the critics who admire. "Here is a picture," they might say, "on whose meaning no two of you are in agreement. Communication between the artist and the spectator has almost completely broken down, for each of you admits that it has broken down as regards every spectator except himself. There are only two possible explanations. Either the artist was a very bad artist, or you are very bad critics. In deference to your number and your reputation, we choose the first alternative; though, as you will observe, it would work out to the same result if we chose the second." As to the next group—those who denied that there was anything odd about the central figure—I believe that in the circumstances I have imagined we should hardly attend to them. A natural and self-explanatory pose in the central figure would be rejected as wholly inconsistent with its observed effect on all the other critics, both those who thought the picture good and those who thought it bad.

If we now return to the real situation, the same reactions appear reasonable. There is, indeed, this difference, that the critics who admit no delay and no indecision in Hamlet, have an opponent with whom the corresponding critics of the picture were not embarrassed. The picture did not answer back. But Hamlet does. He pronounces himself a procrastinator, an undecided man, even a coward: and the ghost in part agrees with him. This, coupled with the more general difficulties of their position, appears to me to be fatal to their view. If so, we are left with those who think the play bad and those who agree in thinking it good and in placing its goodness almost wholly in the character of the hero, while disagreeing as to what that character is. Surely the devil's advocates are in a very strong position. Here is a play so dominated by one character that "*Hamlet* without the Prince" is a byword. Here are critics justly famed, all of them for their sensibility, many of them for their skill in catching the finest shades of human passion and pursuing motives to their last hiding-places. Is it really credible that the greatest of dramatists, the most powerful painter of men, offering to such an audience his consummate portrait of a man should produce something which, if any one of them is right, all the rest have in some degree failed to recognise? Is this the sort of thing that happens? Does the meeting of supremely creative with supremely receptive imagination usually produce such results? Or is it not far easier to say that Homer nods, and Alexander's shoulder drooped, and Achilles' heel was vulnerable, and that Shakespeare, for once, either in haste, or over-reaching himself in unhappy ingenuity, has brought forth an abortion?

Yes. Of course it is far easier. "Most certainly," says Mr. Eliot, "an artistic failure." But is it "most certain"? Let me return for a moment to my analogy of the picture. In that dream there was one experiment we did not make. We didn't walk into the next room and look at it for ourselves. Supposing we had done so. Suppose that at the first glance all the cogent arguments of the unfavourable critics had died on our lips, or echoed in our ears as idle babble. Suppose that looking on the picture we had found ourselves caught up into an unforgettable intensity of life and had come back from the room where it hung haunted for ever with the sense of vast dignities and strange sorrows and teased "with thoughts beyond the reaches of our souls"—would not this have reversed our judgement and compelled us, in the teeth of *a priori* probability, to maintain that on one point at least the ortho-dox critics were in the right? "Most certainly an artistic failure." All argument is for that conclusion—until you read or see *Hamlet* again. And when you do, you are left saying that if this is failure, then failure is better than success. We want more of these "bad" plays. From our first childish reading of the ghost scenes down to those golden minutes which we stole from marking examination papers on *Hamlet* to read a few pages of *Hamlet* itself, have we ever known the day or the hour when its enchantment failed? That castle is part of our own world. The affection we feel for the Prince, and, through him, for Horatio, is like a friendship in real life. The very turns of expression—half-lines and odd connecting links—of this play are worked into the language. It appears, said Shaftesbury in 1710, "most to have affected English hearts and has perhaps been oftenest acted." It has a taste of its own, an all-pervading relish which we recognise even in its smallest frag-ments, and which, once tasted, we recur to. When we want that taste, no other book will do instead. It may turn out in the end that the thing is not a complete success. This compelling quality in it may coexist with some radical defect. But I doubt if we shall ever be able to say, sad brow and true maid, that it is "most cer-tainly" a failure. Even if the proposition that it has failed were at last admitted for true, I can think of few critical truths which most of us would utter with less certainty, and with a more divided mind.

It seems, then, that we cannot escape from our problem by pronouncing the play bad. On the other hand, the critics, mostly agreeing to place the excellence of it in the delineation of the hero's character, describe that character in a dozen different ways. If they differ so much as to the kind of man whom Shakespeare meant to portray, how can we explain their unanimous praise of the portrayal? I can imagine a sketch so bad that one man thought it was an attempt at a horse and another thought it was an attempt at a donkey. But what kind of sketch would it have to be which looked like a *very good* horse to some, and like a *very good* donkey to others? The only solution which occurs to me is that the critics' delight in the play is not in fact due to the delineation of Hamlet's character but to something else. If the picture which you take for a horse and I for a donkey, delights us both, it is probable that what we are both enjoying is the pure line, or the colouring, not the delineation of an animal. If two men who have both been talking to the same woman agree in proclaiming her conversation delightful, though one praises it for its ingenuous innocence and the other for its clever sophistication, I should be inclined to conclude that her conversation had played very little part in the pleasure of either. I should suspect that the lady was nice to look at.

I am quite aware that such a suggestion about what has always been thought a "one man play" will sound rather like a paradox. But I am not aiming at singularity. In so far as my own ideas about Shakespeare are worth classifying at all, I confess myself a member of that school which has lately been withdrawing our attention from the characters to fix it on the plays. Dr. Stoll and Professor Wilson Knight, though in very different fashions, have led me in this direction; and Aristotle has long seemed to me simply right when he says that tragedy is an imitation not of men but of action and life and happiness and misery. By action he means, no doubt, not what a modern producer would call action but rather "situation".

What has attached me to this way of thinking is the fact that it explains my own experience. When I tried to read Shakespeare in my teens the character criticism of the nineteenth century stood between me and my enjoyment. There were all sorts of things in the plays which I could have enjoyed; but I had got it into my head that the only proper and grown-up way of appreciating Shakespeare was to be very interested in the truth and subtlety of his character drawing. A play opened with thunder and lightning and witches on a heath. This was very much in my line: but oh the disenchantment when I was told—or thought I was told —that what really ought to concern me was the effect of these witches on Macbeth's character! An Illyrian Duke spoke, in an air which had just ceased vibrating to the sound of music, words that seemed to come out of the very heart of some golden world of dreamlike passion: but all this was spoiled because the meddlers had told me it was the portrait of a self-deceiving or unrealistic man and given me the impression that it was my business to diagnose like a straightener from Erewhon or Vienna instead of submitting to the charm. Shakespeare offered me a King who could not even sentence a man to banishment without saying:

> The sly slow hours shall not determinate
> The dateless limit of thy dear exile.

Left to myself I would simply have drunk it in and been thankful. That is just how beautiful, wilful, passionate, unfortunate kings killed long ago ought to talk. But then again the critic was at my elbow instilling the pestilential notion that I ought to prize such words chiefly as illustrations of what he called Richard's weakness, and (worse still) inviting me to admire the vulgar, bustling efficiency of Bolingbroke. I am probably being very unjust to the critics in this account. I am not even sure who they were. But somehow or other this was the sort of idea they gave me. I believe they have given it to thousands. As far as I am concerned it meant that Shakespeare became to me for many years a closed book. Read him in *that* way I could not; and it was some time before I had the courage to read him in any other. Only much later, reinforced with a wider knowledge of literature, and able now to rate at its true value the humble little outfit of prudential maxims which really underlay much of the talk about Shakespeare's characters, did I return and read him with enjoyment. To one in my position the opposite movement in criticism came as a kind of Magna Carta. With that help I have come to one very definite conclusion. I do not say that the characters—especially the comic characters—count for nothing. But the first thing is to surrender oneself to the poetry and the situation. It is only through them that you can reach the characters, and it is for their sake that the characters exist. All conceptions of the characters arrived at, so to speak, in cold blood, by working out what sort of man it would have to be who in real life would act or speak as they do, are in my opinion chimerical. The wiseacres who proceed in that way only substitute our own ideas of character and life, which are not often either profound or delectable, for the bright shapes which the poet is actually using. Orsino and Richard II are test cases. Interpretations which compel you to read their speeches with a certain superiority, to lend them a note of "insincerity", to strive in any way against their beauty, are self-condemned. Poets do not make beautiful verse in order to have it "guyed". Both these characters speak golden syllables, wearing rich clothes, and standing in the centre of the stage. After that, they may be wicked, but it can only be with a passionate and poetic wickedness; they may be foolish, but only with follies noble and heroical. For the poetry, the clothes, and the stance are the substance; the character "as it would have to be in real life" is only a shadow. It is often a very distorted shadow. Some of my pupils talk to me about Shakespeare as if the object of his life had been to render into verse the philosophy of Samuel Smiles or Henry Ford.

A good example of the kind of play which can be twisted out of recognition by character criticism is the *Merchant of Venice*. Nothing is easier than to disengage and condemn the mercenary element in Bassanio's original suit to Portia, to point out that Jessica was a bad daughter, and by dwelling on Shylock's wrongs to turn him into a tragic figure. The hero thus becomes a scamp, the heroine's love for him a disaster, the villain a hero, the last act an irrelevance, and the casket story a monstrosity. What is not explained is why anyone should enjoy such a depressing and confused piece of work. It seems to me that what we actually enjoy is something quite different. The real play is not so much about men as about metals. The horror of usury lay in the fact that it treated metal in a way contrary to nature. If you have cattle they will breed. To make money—the mere medium of exchange—breed as if it were alive is a sort of black magic. The speech about Laban and Jacob is put into Shylock's mouth to show that he cannot grasp this distinction; and the Christians point out that friendship does not take "a breed of barren metal". The important thing about Bassanio is that he can say, "Only my blood speaks to you in my veins", and again, "All the wealth I had ran in my veins." Sir Walter Raleigh most unhappily, to my mind, speaks of Bassanio as a "pale shadow". *Pale* is precisely the wrong word. The whole contrast is between the crimson and organic wealth in his veins, the medium of nobility and fecundity, and the cold, mineral wealth in Shylock's counting-house. The charge that he is a mercenary wooer is a product of prosaic analysis. The play is much nearer the *Märchen* level than that. When the hero marries the princess we are not expected to ask whether her wealth, her beauty, or her rank was the determining factor. They are all blended together in the simple man's conception of Princess. Of course great ladies are beautiful: of course they are rich. Bassanio compares Portia to the Golden Fleece. That strikes the proper note. And when once we approach the play with our senses and imaginations it becomes obvious that the presence of the casket story is no accident. For it also is a story about metals, and the rejection of the commercial metals by Bassanio is a kind of counterpoint to the conquest of Shylock's metallic power by the lady of the beautiful mountain. The very terms in which they are rejected proclaim it. Silver is the "pale and common drudge 'twixt man and man". Gold is "hard food for Midas"—Midas who, like

Shylock, tried to use as the fuel of life what is in its own nature dead. And the last act, so far from being an irrelevant *coda*, is almost the thing for which the play exists. The "naughty world" of finance exists in the play chiefly that we may perceive the light of the "good deed", or rather of the good state, which is called Belmont. I know that some will call this "far-fetched"; but I must ask them to take my word for it that even if I am wrong, "far-fetched" is the last epithet that should be applied to my error. I have not fetched it from far. This, or something like it, is my immediate and spontaneous reaction. A wicked ogre of a Jew is ten thousand miles nearer to that reaction than any of the sad, subtle, realistic figures produced by critics. If I err, I err in childishness, not in sophistication.

Now *Hamlet* is a play as nearly opposite to the *Merchant* as possible. A good way of introducing you to my experience of it will be to tell you the exact point at which anyone else's criticism of it begins to lose my allegiance. It is a fairly definite point. As soon as I find anyone treating the ghost merely as the means whereby Hamlet learns of his father's murder—as soon as a critic leaves us with the impression that some other method of disclosure (the finding of a letter or a conversation with a servant) would have done very nearly as well—I part company with that critic. After that, he may be as learned and sensitive as you please; but his outlook on literature is so remote from mine that he can teach me nothing. Hamlet for me is no more separable from his ghost than Macbeth from his witches, Una from her lion, or Dick Whittington from his cat. The Hamlet formula, so to speak, is not "a man who has to avenge his father" but "a man who has been given a task by a ghost". Everything else about him is less important than that. If the play did not begin with the cold and darkness and sickening suspense of the ghost scenes it would be a radically different play. If, on the other hand, only the first act had survived, we should have a very tolerable notion of the play's

61

peculiar quality. I put it to you that everyone's imagination here confirms mine. What is against me is the abstract pattern of motives and characters which we build up as critics when the actual flavour or tint of the poetry is already fading from our minds.

This ghost is different from any other ghost in Elizabethan drama—for, to tell the truth, the Elizabethans in general do their ghosts very vilely. It is permanently ambiguous. Indeed the very word "ghost", by putting it into the same class with the "ghosts" of Kyd and Chapman, nay by classifying it at all, puts us on the wrong track. It is "this thing", "this dreaded sight", an "illusion", a "spirit of health or goblin damn'd", liable at any moment to assume "some other horrible form" which reason could not survive the vision of. Critics have disputed whether Hamlet is sincere when he doubts whether the apparition is his father's ghost or not. I take him to be perfectly sincere. He believes while the thing is present: he doubts when it is away. Doubt, uncertainty, bewilderment to almost any degree, is what the ghost creates not only in Hamlet's mind but in the minds of the other characters. Shakespeare does not take the concept of "ghost" for granted, as other dramatists had done. In his play the appearance of the spectre means a breaking down of the walls of the world and the germination of thoughts that cannot really be thought: chaos is come again.

This does not mean that I am going to make the ghost the hero, or the play a ghost story—though I might add that a very good ghost story would be, to me, a more interesting thing than a maze of motives. I have started with the ghost because the ghost appears at the beginning of the play not only to give Hamlet necessary information but also, and even more, to strike the note. From the platform we pass to the court scene and so to Hamlet's first long speech. There are ten lines of it before we reach what is necessary to the plot: lines about the melting of flesh into a dew and the divine prohibition of self-slaughter. We have a second ghost scene after which the play itself, rather than the hero, goes mad for some minutes. We have a second soliloquy on the theme "to die . . . to sleep", and a third on "the witching time of night, when churchyards yawn". We have the King's effort to pray and Hamlet's comment on it. We have the ghost's third appearance. Ophelia goes mad and is drowned. Then comes the comic relief, surely the strangest comic relief ever written—comic relief beside an open grave, with a further discussion of suicide, a detailed inquiry into the rate of decomposition, a few clutches of skulls, and then "Alas, poor Yorick!" On top of this, the hideous fighting in the grave; and then, soon, the catastrophe.

I said just now that the subject of the *Merchant* was metals. In the same sense, the subject of *Hamlet* is death. I do not mean by this that most of the characters die, nor even that life and death are the stakes they play for; that is true of all tragedies. I do not mean that we rise from the reading of the play with the feeling that we have been in cold, empty places, places "outside", *nocte tacentia late*, though that is true. Before I go on to explain myself let me say that here, and throughout my lecture, I am most deeply indebted to my friend Mr. Owen Barfield. I have to make these acknowledgements both to him and to other of my friends so often that I am afraid of their being taken for an affectation. But they are not. The next best thing to being wise oneself is to live in a circle of those who are: that good fortune I have enjoyed for nearly twenty years.

The sense in which death is the subject of *Hamlet* will become apparent if we compare it with other plays. Macbeth has commerce with Hell, but at the very outset of his career dismisses all thought of the life to come. For Brutus and Othello, suicide in the high tragic manner is escape and climax. For Lear death is deliverance. For Romeo and Antony, poignant loss. For all these, as for their author while he writes and the audience while they watch, death is the end: it is almost the frame of the picture. They think of dying: no one thinks, in these plays, of *being dead*. In *Hamlet* we are kept thinking about it all the time, whether in terms of the soul's destiny or of the body's. Purgatory, Hell, Heaven, the wounded name, the rights—or wrongs—of Ophelia's burial, and the staying-power of a tanner's corpse: and beyond this, beyond all Christian and all Pagan maps of the hereafter, comes a curious groping and tapping of thoughts, about "what dreams may come". It is this that gives to the whole play its quality of darkness and of misgiving. Of course there is much else in the play: but nearly always, the same groping. The characters are all watching one another, forming theories about one another, listening, contriving, full of anxiety. The world of *Hamlet* is a world where one has lost one's way. The Prince also has no doubt lost his, and we can tell the precise moment at which he finds it again. "Not a whit. We defy augury. There's a special providence in the fall of a sparrow. If it be now, 'tis not to come: if it be not to come, it will be now: if it be not now, yet it will come: the readiness is all: since no man has aught of what he leaves, what is't to leave betimes?"[1]

If I wanted to make one more addition to the gallery of Hamlet's portraits I should trace his hesitation to the fear of death; not to a physical fear of dying, but a fear of being dead. And I think I should get on quite comfortably. Any serious attention to the state of being dead, unless it is limited by some definite religious or anti-religious doctrine, must, I suppose, paralyse the will by introducing infinite uncertainties and rendering all motives inadequate. Being dead is the unknown x in our sum. Unless you ignore it or else give it a value, you can get no answer. But this

---

[1] I think the last clause is best explained by the assumption that Shakespeare had come across Seneca's *Nihil perdis ex tuo tempore, nam quod relinquis alienum est* (Epist. lxix).

is not what I am going to do. Shakespeare has not left in the text clear lines of causation which would enable us to connect Hamlet's hesitation with this source. I do not believe he has given us data for any portrait of the kind critics have tried to draw. To that extent I agree with Hanmer, Rümelin, and Mr. Eliot. But I differ from them in thinking that it is a fault.

For what, after all, is happening to us when we read any of Hamlet's great speeches? We see visions of the flesh dissolving into a dew, of the world like an unweeded garden. We think of memory reeling in its "distracted globe". We watch him scampering hither and thither like a maniac to avoid the voices wherewith he is haunted. Someone says "Walk out of the air", and we hear the words "Into my grave" spontaneously respond to it. We think of being bounded in a nut-shell and king of infinite space: but for bad dreams. There's the trouble, for "I am most dreadfully attended". We see the picture of a dull and muddy-mettled rascal, a John-a-dreams, somehow unable to move while ultimate dishonour is done him. We listen to his fear lest the whole thing may be an illusion due to melancholy. We get the sense of sweet relief at the words "shuffled off this mortal coil" but mixed with the bottomless doubt about what may follow then. We think of bones and skulls, of women breeding sinners, and of how some, to whom all this experience is a sealed book, can yet dare death and danger "for an eggshell". But do we really enjoy these things, do we go back to them, because they show us Hamlet's character? Are they, from *that* point of view, so very interesting? Does the mere fact that a young man, literally haunted, dispossessed, and lacking friends, should feel thus, tell us anything remarkable? Let me put my question in another way. If instead of the speeches he actually utters about the firmament and man in his scene with Rosencrantz and Guildenstern Hamlet had merely said, "I don't seem to enjoy things the way I used to", and talked in that fashion throughout, should we find him interesting? I think the answer is "Not very". It may be replied that if he talked commonplace prose he would reveal his character less vividly. I am not so sure. He would certainly have revealed *something* less vividly; but would that something be himself? It seems to me that "this majestical roof" and "What a piece of work is a man" give me primarily an impression not of the sort of person he must be to lose the estimation of things but of the things themselves and their great value; and that I should be able to discern, though with very faint interest, the same condition of loss in a personage who was quite unable so to put before me what he was losing. And I do not think it true to reply that he would be a different character if he spoke less poetically. This point is often misunderstood. We sometimes speak as if the characters in whose mouths Shakespeare puts great poetry were poets: in the sense that Shakespeare was depicting men of poetical genius. But surely this is like thinking that Wagner's Wotan is the dramatic portrait of a baritone? In opera song is the medium by which the representation is made and not part of the thing represented. The actors sing; the dramatic personages are feigned to be speaking. The only character who sings dramatically in *Figaro* is Cherubino. Similarly in poetical drama poetry is the medium, not part of the delineated characters. While the actors speak poetry written for them by the poet, the dramatic personages are supposed to be merely talking. If ever there is occasion to *represent* poetry (as in the play scene from *Hamlet*), it is put into a different metre and strongly stylised so as to prevent confusion.

I trust that my conception is now becoming clear. I believe that we read Hamlet's speeches with interest chiefly because they describe so well a certain spiritual region through which most of us have passed and anyone in his circumstances might be expected to pass, rather than because of our concern to understand how and why this particular man entered it. I foresee an objection on the ground that I am thus really admitting his "character" in the only sense that matters and that all characters whatever could be equally well talked away by the method I have adopted. But I do really find a distinction. When I read about Mrs. Proudie I am not in the least interested in seeing the world from her point of view, for her point of view is not interesting; what does interest me is precisely the sort of person she was. In *Middlemarch* no reader wants to see Casaubon through Dorothea's eyes; the pathos, the comedy, the value of the whole thing is to understand Dorothea and see how such an illusion was inevitable for her. In Shakespeare himself I find Beatrice to be a character who could not be thus dissolved. We are interested not in some vision seen through her eyes, but precisely in the wonder of her being the girl she is. A comparison of the sayings we remember from her part with those we remember from Hamlet's brings out the contrast. On the one hand, "I wonder that you will still be talking, Signior Benedick", "There was a star danced and under that I was born", "Kill Claudio"; on the other, "The undiscovered country from whose bourne no traveller returns", "Use every man after his desert, and who should 'scape whipping?", "The rest is silence". Particularly noticeable is the passage where Hamlet professes to be describing his own character. "I am myself indifferent honest: but yet I could accuse me of such things that it were better my mother had not borne me. I am very proud, revengeful, ambitious." It is, of course, possible to devise some theory which explains these self-accusations in terms of character. But long before we have done so the real significance of the lines has taken possession of our imagination for ever. "Such fellows as I" does not mean "such fellows as Goethe's Hamlet, or Coleridge's Hamlet, or any Hamlet": it means *men*—creatures shapen in sin and conceived in iniquity—and the vast, empty vision of them "crawling between earth and heaven" is what really counts and really carries the burden of the play.

It is often cast in the teeth of the great critics that each in painting *Hamlet* has drawn a portrait of himself. How if they were right? I would go a long way to meet Beatrice or Falstaff or Mr. Jonathan Oldbuck or Disraeli's Lord Monmouth. I would not cross the room to meet Hamlet. It would never be necessary. He is always where I am. The method of the whole play is much nearer to Mr. Eliot's own method in poetry than Mr. Eliot suspects. Its true hero is man—haunted man—man with his mind on the frontier of two worlds, man unable either quite to reject or quite to admit the supernatural, man struggling to get something done as man has struggled from the beginning, yet incapable of achievement because of his inability to understand either himself or his fellows or the real quality of the universe which has produced him. To be sure, some hints of more particular motives for Hamlet's delay are every now and then fadged up to silence our questions, just as some show of motives is offered for the Duke's temporary abdication in *Measure for Measure*. In both cases it is only scaffolding or machinery. To mistake these mere *succedanea* for the real play and to try to work them up into a coherent psychology is the great error. I once had a whole batch of School Certificate answers on the Nun's Priest's Tale by boys whose form-master was apparently a breeder of poultry. Everything that Chaucer had said in describing Chauntecleer and Pertelote was treated by them simply and solely as evidence about the precise breed of these two birds. And, I must admit, the result was very interesting. They proved beyond doubt that Chauntecleer was very different from our modern specialised strains and much closer to the Old English "barn-door fowl". But I couldn't help feeling that they had missed something. I believe our attention to Hamlet's "character" in the usual sense misses almost as much.

Perhaps I should rather say that it *would* miss as much if our behaviour when we are actually reading were not wiser than our criticism in cold blood. The critics, or most of them, have at any rate kept constantly before us the knowledge that in this play there is greatness and mystery. They were never entirely wrong. Their error, on my view, was to put the mystery in the wrong place—in Hamlet's motives rather than in that darkness which enwraps Hamlet and the whole tragedy and all who read or watch it. It is a mysterious play in the sense of being a play about mystery. Mr. Eliot suggests that "more people have thought *Hamlet* a work of art because they found it interesting, than have found it interesting because it is a work of art". When he wrote that sentence he must have been very near to what I believe to be the truth. This play is, above all else, *interesting*. But artistic failure is not in itself interesting, nor often interesting in any way; artistic success always is. To interest is the first duty of art; no other excellences will even begin to compensate for failure in this, and very serious faults will be covered by this, as by charity. The hypothesis that this play interests by being good and not by being bad has therefore the first claim on our consideration. The burden of proof rests on the other side. Is not the fascinated interest of the critics most naturally explained by supposing that this is the precise effect the play was written to produce? They may be finding the mystery in the wrong place; but the fact that they can never leave *Hamlet* alone, the continual groping, the sense, unextinguished by over a century of failures, that we have here something of inestimable importance, is surely the best evidence that the real and lasting mystery of our human situation has been greatly depicted.

The kind of criticism which I have attempted is always at a disadvantage against either historical criticism or character criticism. Their vocabulary has been perfected by long practice, and the truths with which they are concerned are those which we are accustomed to handle in the everyday business of life. But the things I want to talk about have no vocabulary and criticism has for centuries kept almost complete silence on them. I make no claim to be a pioneer. Professor Wilson Knight (though I disagree with nearly everything he says in detail), Miss Spurgeon, Miss Bodkin, and Mr. Barfield are my leaders. But those who do not enjoy the honours of a pioneer may yet share his discomforts. One of them I feel acutely at the moment. I feel certain that to many of you the things I have been saying about *Hamlet* will appear intolerably sophisticated, abstract, and modern. And so they sound when we have to put them into words. But I shall have failed completely if I cannot persuade you that my view, for good or ill, has just the opposite characteristics—is naïve and concrete and archaic. I am trying to recall attention from the things an intellectual adult notices to the things a child or a peasant notices —night, ghosts, a castle, a lobby where a man can walk four hours together, a willow-fringed brook and a sad lady drowned, a graveyard and a terrible cliff above the sea, and amidst all these a pale man in black clothes (would that our producers would ever let him appear!) with his stockings coming down, a dishevelled man whose words make us at once think of loneliness and doubt and dread, of waste and dust and emptiness, and from whose hands, or from our own, we feel the richness of heaven and earth and the comfort of human affection slipping away. In a sense I have kept my promise of bestowing all my childishness upon you. A child is always thinking about those details in a story which a grown-up regards as indifferent. If when you first told the tale your hero was warned by three little men appearing on the left of the road, and when you tell it again you introduce one little man on the right of the road, the child protests. And the child is right. You think it makes no difference because you are not living the story at all. If you were, you would know better. *Motifs*, machines, and the like are abstractions of literary history and therefore interchangeable: but concrete imagination knows nothing of them.

Hamlet: The Prince or The Poem?

You must not think I am setting up as a sort of literary Peter Pan who does not grow up. On the contrary, I claim that only those adults who have retained, with whatever additions and enrichments, their first childish response to poetry unimpaired, can be said to have grown up at all. Mere change is not growth. Growth is the synthesis of change and continuity, and where there is no continuity there is no growth. To hear some critics, one would suppose that a man had to lose his nursery appreciation of *Gulliver* before he acquired his mature appreciation of it. It is not so. If it were, the whole concept of maturity, of ripening, would be out of place: and also, I believe we should very seldom read more than three pages of *Gulliver* at a sitting.

The Annual Shakespeare Lecture of the British Academy, 1942

4

Kipling's World

KIPLING IS intensely loved and hated. Hardly any reader likes him a little. Those who admire him will defend him tooth and nail, and resent unfavourable criticism of him as if he were a mistress or a country rather than a writer. The other side reject him with something like personal hatred. The reason is not hard to find and will, I hope, become apparent as we go on. For the moment, I will only say that I do not fully belong to either side.

I have been reading him off and on all my life, and I never return to him without renewed admiration. I have never at any time been able to understand how a man of taste could doubt that Kipling is a very great artist. On the other hand, I have never quite taken him to my heart. He is not one of my indispensables; life would go on much the same if the last copy of his works disappeared. I can go even further than this. Not only is my allegiance imperfect, it is also inconstant. After I have been reading Kipling for some days together there comes a sudden check. One moment I am filled with delight at the variety and solidity of his imagination; and then, at the very next moment, I am sick, sick to death, of the whole Kipling world. Of course, one can reach temporary saturation point with any author; there comes an evening when even Boswell or Virgil will do no longer. But one parts from them as a friend: one knows one will want them another day; and in the interval one thinks of them with pleasure. But I mean something quite different from that; I mean a real disenchantment, a recoil which makes the Kipling world

72

for the moment, not dull (it is never that), but unendurable—a heavy, glaring, suffocating monstrosity. It is the difference between feeling that, on the whole, you would not like another slice of bread and butter just now, and wondering, as your gorge rises, how you could ever have imagined that you liked vodka.

I by no means assume that this sudden change of feeling is reasonable. But it must certainly have causes, and I hope that to explore them may cast some light on Kipling. I am going to suggest that they are two in number, one arising from what may be called the formal, the other from what may be called the material, character of his work. I admit that this distinction of form from matter breaks down if you press it too far, or in certain directions, but I think it will do for the purpose I have in hand.

The first cause for my sudden recoil from Kipling, I take to be not the defect but the excess of his art. He himself has told us how he licked every story into its final shape. He dipped a brush in Indian ink and then re-read the manuscript "in an auspicious hour", considering faithfully "every paragraph, sentence and word" and "blacking out where requisite". After a time he re-read the story and usually found that it would bear "a second shortening". Finally there came a third reading at which still more deletion might or might not be found necessary.[1] It is a magnificent example of self-discipline, which Horace would have approved. But I suggest that even an athlete can be over-trained. Superfluous flesh should be sweated off; but a cruel trainer may be too severe in judging what is superfluous. I think Kipling used the Indian ink too much. Sometimes the story has been so compressed that in the completed version it is not quite told—at least, I still do not know exactly what happened in *Mrs. Bathurst*. But even when this is not so, the art overreaches itself in another way. Every sentence that did not seem to Kipling perfectly and triumphantly good has been removed. As a result the style tends

[1] *Autobiography*, Chapter 8.

to be too continuously and obtrusively brilliant. The result is a little fatiguing. Our author gives us no rest: we are bombarded with felicities till they deafen us. There is no elbow room, no leisureliness. We need roughage as well as nourishment in a diet; but there is no roughage in a Kipling story—it is all unrelieved vitamins from the first word to the last.

To this criticism I think Kipling could make an almost perfectly satisfactory answer. He might say that he was writing short stories and short poems, each of which was to be the only specimen of Kipling in some number of a periodical. His work was meant to be taken in small doses. The man who gobbles down one story after another at a sitting has no more right to complain if the result is disastrous than the man who swills liqueurs as if they were beer. This answer, I have said, seems to me almost complete. Almost—because even inside a single story the brilliance of the parts, in my opinion, sometimes damages the effect of the whole. I am thinking of *My Sunday at Home*. The fancied situation is excellent; one ought to remember the story with chuckles as one remembers *The Wrong Box*. But I know I am not alone in finding that one actually laughed less than one would have thought possible in the reading of it and that in remembering it one always reverts to the summer drowsiness of the Wiltshire country around the railway station. That superb piece of scene painting has almost blotted out the comic action. Yet I suppose it was originally introduced for no other purpose than to emphasise the solitude of the place.

The fault of which I am here accusing Kipling is one which only a great artist could commit. For most of us the old rule of cutting out every word that can be spared is still a safe one: there is no danger that even after this process the result will be too vivid and too full of sense. And, as far as mere art is concerned, I think this is almost the only fault I can find in Kipling's mature work; I say his mature work for, of course, like all men he made some unsuccessful experiments before he found his true vein. It is when I turn to his matter that my serious discontents begin.

The earliest generation of Kipling's readers regarded him as the mouthpiece of patriotism and imperialism. I think that conception of his work is inadequate. Chesterton did a great service to criticism by contradicting it in a famous chapter of *Heretics*. In that chapter he finds the essential characteristics of Kipling's mind to be two. In the first place he had discovered, or rediscovered, the poetry of common things; had perceived, as Chesterton says, "the significance and philosophy of steam and of slang". In the second place, Kipling was the poet of discipline. Not specially, nor exclusively, of military discipline, but of discipline of every shape. "He has not written so well of soldiers," says Chesterton, "as he has of railwaymen or bridge-builders, or even journalists." This particular judgement may be disputed, but I feel no doubt at all that Chesterton has picked up the right scent.

To put the thing in the shortest possible way, Kipling is first and foremost the poet of work. It is really remarkable how poetry and fiction before his time had avoided this subject. They had dealt almost exclusively with men in their "private hours"— with love-affairs, crimes, sport, illness and changes of fortune. Mr. Osborne may be a merchant, but *Vanity Fair* has no interest in his mercantile life. Darcy was a good landlord and Wentworth a good officer, but their activities in these capacities were all "offstage". Most of Scott's characters, except the soldiers, have no profession; and when they are soldiers the emphasis is on battles and adventures, not on the professional routine. Business comes into Dickens only in so far as it is criminal or comic. With a few exceptions[1] imaginative literature in the eighteenth and nineteenth centuries had quietly omitted, or at least thrust into the background, the sort of thing which in fact occupies most of the waking hours of most men. And this did not merely mean

[1] Of these *Middlemarch* is perhaps the finest.

that certain technical aspects of life were unrepresented. A whole range of strong sentiments and emotions—for many men, the strongest of all—went with them. For, as Pepys once noted with surprise, there is a great pleasure in talking of business. It was Kipling who first reclaimed for literature this enormous territory.

His early stories of Anglo-Indian society still conform to the older convention. They are about love-affairs, elopements, intrigues and domestic quarrels. They are indeed connected with his later and more characteristic work by a thread which I shall discuss presently; but on the surface they are a different kind of thing. The *Departmental Ditties* are much more typical of the author's real interests. The point about Potiphar Gubbins is not simply that he is a cuckold, but that his horns bring him advancement in the Civil Service and that he builds very bad bridges. The sting of *The Story of Uriah* lies not merely in the wife's depravity but in the fact that the husband was sent, for her lover's convenience, to die at Quetta, "attempting two men's duty in that very healthy post". Exeter Battleby Tring, who really knows something about railways, has his mouth silenced with rupees in order that "the Little Tin Gods (long may their Highnesses thrive!)" may keep "their Circle intact". Boanerges Blitzen ruins his official career by exposing "office scandals" in the papers. The whole bitter little collection presents a corrupt society, not in its leisure, but in its official corruption. In his later work this preference for depicting men at their jobs becomes his most obvious characteristic. Findlayson's hopes and fears about his bridge, McPhee's attitude both to engines and owners, William the Conqueror's work in the famine district, a lighthouse-keeper at his post on a foggy night, Gisborne and his chief in the forest, McAndrew standing his watch—these are the things that come back to us when we remember Kipling; and there had really been nothing like them in literature before. The poems again and again strike the same note. Lord Dufferin (heavily influenced by Bishop Blougram) hands on the *arcana imperii* to Lord Lansdowne; the professional spies set out, "each man reporting for duty alone, out of sight, out of reach of his fellow"; the crew of the *Bolivar*, "mad with work and weariness", see "some damned Liner's lights go by like a grand hotel"; H. Mukerji sends with the Boh's head a covering letter in perfect Babu officialese; the fans and beltings in a munition factory roar round a widowed war worker. The rhythms of work—boots slogging along a road, the Harrild and the Hoe devouring "their league-long paper-bale", the grunting of a water-wheel—echo through Kipling's verse and prose as through no other man's. Even Mowgli in the end accepts a post in the Civil Service. Even *The Brushwood Boy* turns aside from its main theme to show how much toil its hero suffered and inflicted in the course of his profession. Even when we are taken into the remote past, Kipling is not interested in imagining what it felt like to be an ancient and pagan man; only in what it felt like to be a man doing some ancient job—a galley slave, a Roman officer. How the light came in through the oar-holes in the galley—that little detail which everyone who had served in a galley would remember and which no one else would know—that is Kipling's quarry.

It would be a mistake, however, to accuse Kipling of swamping the human interest in his mass of material and technical detail. The detail is there for the sake of a human interest, but that human interest is one that no previous writer had done justice to. What Kipling chiefly communicates—and it is, for good and for ill, one of the strongest things in the world—is the peculiar relation which men who do the same work have to that work and to one another; the inescapable bond of shared experiences, and, above all, of shared hardships. It is a commitment for life:

> Oh, was there ever sailor free to choose,
>   That didn't settle somewhere near the sea?
> We've only one virginity to lose,
>   And where we lost it, there our hearts will be.

That is why in *Steam Tactics* Hinchcliffe, who, when starting on his leave, had "thanked his Maker that he wouldn't see nor smell nor thumb a runnin' bulgine till the nineteenth prox", nevertheless fell immediately to studying the engine of Kipling's steam-car.

For the same reason, Kipling, the old journalist, writes:

> But the Jew shall forget Jerusalem
> Ere we forget the Press.

In the next stanza he goes on to explain why. The man who has "stood through the loaded hour" and "lit his pipe in the morning calm"—who has, in fact, been through the nocturnal routine of producing a newspaper—"hath sold his heart". That is the whole point. We who are of one trade (whether journalists, soldiers, galley slaves, Indian Civilians, or what you will) know so many things that the outsiders will never, never understand. Like the two child lovers in *The Light that Failed*, "we belong." It is a bond which in real life sometimes proves stronger than any other:

> The men of my own stock
> They may do ill or well,
> But they tell the lies I am wonted to,
> They are used to the lies I tell;
> And we do not need interpreters
> When we go to buy or sell.

How true to life is the immediate alliance of the three journalists whom chance has thrown together in the story called *A Matter of Fact*.

This spirit of the profession is everywhere shown in Kipling as a ruthless master. That is why Chesterton got in a very large part of the truth when he fixed on discipline as Kipling's main subject. There is nothing Kipling describes with more relish than the process whereby the trade-spirit licks some raw cub into shape.

That is the whole theme of one of his few full-length novels, *Captains Courageous*. It is the theme of *The Centaurs*, and of *Pharaoh and the Sergeant*, and of *The 'Eathen*. It is allegorically expressed in *The Ship that Found Herself*. It is implicit in all the army stories and the sea-stories; indeed, it may be thought that the author turns aside from his narrative rather too often to assure us that Mulvaney was invaluable for "licking the new batch of recruits into shape". Even when we escape into the jungle and the wolf pack we do not escape the Law. Until he has been dis-ciplined—"put through it", licked into shape—a man is, for Kipling, mere raw material. "Gad," says Hitchcock to Findlayson in *The Bridge-Builders*, "what a Cooper's Hill cub I was when I came on the works." And Findlayson muses, "Cub thou wast; assistant thou art." The philosophy of the thing is summed up at the end of *A Walking Delegate* where the yellow horse (an agitator) has asked the old working horse, "Have you no respec' what-ever for the dignity o' our common horsehood?" He gets the reply, "Horse, sonny, is what you start from. We know all about horse here, an' he ain't any high-toned pure-souled child of nature. Horse, plain horse, same ez you, is chock-full o' tricks an' meannesses an' cussednesses an' monkey shines . . . That's horse, an' thet's about his dignity an' the size of his soul 'fore he's been broke an' raw-hided a piece." Reading "man" for "horse", we here have Kipling's doctrine of Man.

This is one of the most important things Kipling has to say and one which he means very seriously, and it is also one of the things which has aroused hatred against him. It amounts to something like a doctrine of original sin, and it is antipathetic to many modern modes of thought. Perhaps even more antipathetic is Kipling's presentation of the "breaking" and "raw-hiding" pro-cess. In *His Private Honour* it turns out to consist of prolonged bullying and incessant abuse; the sort of bullying (as we learn from *The 'Eathen*) which sends grown men off to cry in solitude, followed by the jeers of the old hands. The patient is not allowed to claim any personal rights whatever; there is nothing, according to Kipling, more subversive. To ask for justice is as the sin of witchcraft. The disaster in the poem called *That Day* began with the fact that "every little drummer 'ad 'is rights an' wrongs to mind". In contrast, "My rights," Ortheris answered with deep scorn, "My rights! I ain't a recruity to go whinin' about my rights to this an' my rights to that, just as if I couldn't look after myself. My rights! 'Strewth A'mighty. I'm a man."

Now there is no good whatever in dismissing this part of Kipling's message as if it were not worth powder and shot. There is a truth in it which must be faced before we attempt to find any larger truths which it may exclude. Many who hate Kipling have omitted this preliminary. They feel instinctively that they themselves are just the unlicked or unbroken men whom Kipling condemns; they find the picture intolerable, and the picture of the cure more intolerable still. To escape, they dismiss the whole thing as a mere Fascist or "public school" brutality. But there is no solution along those lines. It may (or may not) be possible to get beyond Kipling's harsh wisdom; but there is no getting beyond a thing without first getting as far. It is a brutal truth about the world that the whole everlasting business of keeping the human race protected and clothed and fed could not go on for twenty-four hours without the vast legion of hard-bitten, technically efficient, not-over-sympathetic men, and without the harsh processes of discipline by which this legion is made. It is a brutal truth that unless a great many people practised the Kipling *ethos* there would be neither security nor leisure for any people to practise a finer *ethos*. As Chesterton admits, "We may fling ourselves into a hammock in a fit of divine carelessness; but we are glad that the maker did not make the hammock in a fit of divine carelessness." In *The Proconsuls*, speaking of those who have actually ruled with a strong hand, Kipling says:

On the stage their act hath framed
For thy sports, O Liberty!
Doubted are they, and defamed
By the tongues their act set free.

It is a true bill, as far as it goes. Unless the Kipling virtues—if you
will, the Kipling vices—had long and widely been practised in
the world we should be in no case to sit here and discuss Kipling.
If all men stood talking of their rights before they went up a
mast or down a sewer or stoked a furnace or joined an army,
we should all perish; nor while they talked of their rights would
they learn to do these things. And I think we must agree with
Kipling that the man preoccupied with his own rights is not
only a disastrous, but a very unlovely object; indeed, one of the
worst mischiefs we do by treating a man unjustly is that we
force him to be thus preoccupied.

But if so, then it is all the more important that men should in
fact be treated with justice. If we all need "licking into shape"
and if, while undergoing the process, we must not guard our
rights, then it is all the more important that someone else should
guard them for us. What has Kipling to say on this subject? For,
quite clearly, the very same methods which he prescribes for
licking the cub into shape, "making a man of him" in the interests of the community, would also, if his masters were bad
men, be an admirable method of keeping the cub quiet while he
was exploited and enslaved for their private benefit. It is all very
well that the colts (in the *Centaurs*) should learn to obey Chiron
as a means to becoming good cavalry chargers; but how if Chiron
wants their obedience only to bring them to the knacker's yard?
And are the masters never bad men? From some stories one
would almost conclude that Kipling is ignorant of, or indifferent
to, this possibility. In *His Private Honour* the old soldiers educate
the recruits by continued bullying. But Kipling seems quite unaware that bullying is an activity which human beings *enjoy*. We

are given to understand that the old soldiers are wholly immune to this temptation; they threaten, mock, and thrash the recruits only from the highest possible motives. Is this naïvety in the author? Can he really be so ignorant? Or does he not care?

He is certainly not ignorant. Most of us begin by regarding Kipling as the panegyrist of the whole imperial system. But we find when we look into the matter that his admiration is reserved for those in the lower positions. These are the "men on the spot": the bearers of the burden; above them we find folly and ignorance; at the centre of the whole thing we find the terrible society of Simla, a provincial smart set which plays frivolously with men's careers and even their lives. The system is rotten at the head, and official advancement may have a *teterrima causa*. Findlayson had to see "months of office work destroyed at a blow when the Government of India at the last moment added two feet to the width of the bridge under the impression that bridges were cut out of paper." The heart-rending death of Orde (one of Kipling's best tragic scenes) is followed by the undoing of his life's work when the ignorant Viceroy sends a Babu to succeed him. In *Tod's Amendment* disaster is averted by a child who knows what all the rulers of India (the "little Tin Gods") do not know. It is interesting to compare *The 'Eathen* with *The Sergeant's Wedding*. In the one, the sergeants are benevolent despots—it is only the softness and selfishness of the recruit that make him think they are cruel tyrants. In the other, we have a sergeant who uses his position to make money by cheating the men. Clearly this sergeant would have just as strong a motive as the good ones for detesting privates who talked about their "rights and wrongs".

All this suggests that the disciplinary system is a very two-edged affair; but this does not in the least shake Kipling's devotion to it. That, he says in effect, is what the world has always been like and always will be like. Even in prehistoric times the astute person

Won a simple Viceroy's praise
Through the toil of other men.

And no one can rebuke more stunningly than Kipling those who
exploit and frustrate the much-enduring "man on the spot":

When the last grim joke is entered
In the big black Book of Jobs,
And Quetta graveyards give again
Their victims to the air,
I shouldn't like to be the man
Who sent Jack Barrett there.

But this makes no difference to the duty of the sufferer. Whatever
corruptions there may be at the top, the work must go on;
frontiers must be protected, epidemics fought, bridges built,
marshes drained, famine relief administered. Protest, however
well grounded, about injustice, and schemes of reform, will never
bring a ship into harbour or a train into the station or sow a field
of oats or quell a riot; and "the unforgiving minute" is upon us
fourteen hundred and forty times a day. This is the truest and
finest element in Kipling; his version of Carlyle's gospel of work.
It has affinities with Piers Plowman's insistence on ploughing his
half-acre. But there are important differences.

The more Kipling convinces us that no plea for justice or
happiness must be allowed to interfere with the job, the more
anxious we become for a reassurance that the work is really
worthy of all the human sacrifices it demands. "The game," he
says, "is more than the player of the game." But perhaps some
games are and some aren't. "And the ship is more than the crew"
—but one would like to know where the ship was going and
why. Was its voyage really useful—or even innocent? We want,
in fact, a doctrine of Ends. Langland could supply one. He knows
how Do Well is connected with Do Bet and Do Best; the ploughing of the half acre is placed in a cosmic context and that context
would enable Langland, in principle, to tell us whether any given
job in the whole universe was true worship or miserable idolatry;

it is here that Kipling speaks with an uncertain voice. For many of the things done by his Civil Servants the necessity is perhaps obvious; but that is not a side of the matter he develops. And he writes with equal relish where the ultimate ends of the work described are much less obvious. Sometimes his choice of sides seems to be quite accidental, even frivolous. When William the Conqueror met a schoolmaster who had to teach the natives the beauties of Wordsworth's *Excursion* she told him, rather unnecessarily, "I like men who do things." Teaching English Literature to natives is not "doing things", and we are meant to despise that schoolmaster. One notes that the editor of the local paper, whom we met a few pages before, is visited with no similar ignominy. Yet it is easy enough to imagine the situations reversed. Kipling could have written a perfect Kipling story about two men in the Educational Department working eighteen hours a day to conduct an examination, with punkah flapping and all the usual background. The futility of the curriculum which makes them set Wordsworth to Indian schoolboys would not in the least have detracted from their heroism if he had chosen to write the story from that point of view. It would have been their professional grievance—ironically and stoically endured—one more instance of that irresponsible folly at the top which wastes and breaks the men who really do the work. I have a disquieting feeling that Kipling's actual respect for the journalist and contempt for the schoolmaster has no thought-out doctrine of ends behind it, but results from the accident that he himself worked for a newspaper and not for a school. And now, at last, I begin to suspect that we are finding a clue to that suffocating sensation which overtakes me if I read Kipling too long. Is the Kipling world really monstrous in the sense of being misshaped? How if this doctrine of work and discipline, which is so clear and earnest and dogmatic at the periphery, hides at the centre a terrible vagueness, a frivolity or scepticism?

Sometimes it hides nothing but what the English, whether fairly or unfairly, are inclined to call Americanism. The story called *Below the Mill Dam* is an instance. We are expected to rejoice that the native black rat should be superseded by the alien brown rat; that the mill wheel could be yoked to a dynamo and the countryside electrified. None of the questions which every thinking man must raise about the beneficence of this whole transition have any meaning for Kipling. They are to him mere excuses for idleness. "We have already learned six refined synonyms for loafing," say the waters; and, to the Wheel itself, "while you're at work you'll work." The black rat is to be stuffed. Here is the creed of Activism—of "Progress", hustle, and development—all blind, naked, uncritical of itself. Similarly in *The Explorer*, while we admire the man's courage in the earlier stanzas, the end which he has in view gives us pause. His Holy Grail is simply the industrialisation of the country he has discovered. The waterfalls are "wasting fifty thousand head an hour" and the forests are "axe-ripe"; he will rectify this. The End, here as in the Mill Dam story, may be a good one; it is not for me to decide. But Kipling does not seem to know there is any question. In *Bread upon the Waters* all the usual hardships are described and with all Kipling's usual relish; but the only end is money and revenge—though I confess, a very excusable revenge. In *The Devil and the Deep Sea* the job, which is treated with his usual reverence, the game, which is still more than the player of the game, is merely the triumph of a gang of criminals.

This might be explained by saying that Kipling is not a moralist but a purely objective writer. But that would be false. He is eminently a moralist; in almost every story we are invited, nay forced, to admire and condemn. Many of the poems are versified homilies. That is why this chanciness or uncertainty about the End to which the moralism of his *bushido* is applied in any particular instance makes us uncomfortable. And now we must take

85

a step farther. Even Discipline is not a constant. The very people who would be cubs to be licked into shape in one story may, in another, be the heroes we are asked to admire.

Stalky and his friends are inveterate breakers of discipline. How easily, had his own early memories been different, could Kipling have written the story the other way round. In *Their Lawful Occasions* Moorshed, because he is rich and able to leave the navy next year, can afford to take an independent line. All Kipling's sympathy is with him and against the ship which is significantly named *H.M.S. Pedantic*. Yet Kipling need only have altered the lighting (so to speak) to make Moorshed, and the grounds of his independence, particularly odious and the odium would have been of a characteristically Kiplingese kind. In *Without Benefit of Clergy* Holden's inefficiency as a civil servant is made light of; but had Kipling written in a different mood the very cause of this inefficiency—namely keeping a native mistress —would have been made into a despicable aggravation. In the actual story it is almost an excuse. In *The Germ Destroyer* we actually find Kipling laughing at a man because he has "a marked passion for work!" In *The Bisara of Pooree* that whole Anglo-Indian world, whose work for the natives elsewhere seems so necessary and valuable, is contrasted with the natives as "the shiny, top-scum stuff that people call civilisation". In the *Dream of Duncan Parrenness,* the apparition offers the hero success in the Anglo-Indian career in return for his Trust in Man, his Faith in Woman, and his Boy's Conscience. He gives them all and receives in return "a little piece of dry bread". Where is now the Kipling we thought we knew—the prophet of work, the activist, the writer of *If*? "Were it not better done as others use . . . ?"

You may say that some of these examples are taken from early stories; perhaps Kipling held these sceptical views in his youth and abandoned them in his maturity. Perhaps—as I once half-believed myself—he is a "lost leader" ; a great opposition writer who was somehow caught by government. I think there was a change in his views, but I do not think that goes to the root of the matter. I think that nearly all his work (for there are a few, and very valuable exceptions), at all periods is dominated by one master passion. What he loves better than anything in the world is the intimacy within a closed circle—even if it be only a circle of shared misery as in *In the Same Boat*, or of shared crime as in *The Devil and the Deep Sea*. In the last resort I do not think he loves professional brotherhood for the sake of the work; I think he loves work for the sake of professional brotherhood. Out of that passion all his apparently contradictory moods arise. But I must attempt to define the passion itself a little more closely and to show how it has such a diversified offspring.

When we forgather with three or four trusted cronies of our own calling, a strong sense of community arises and is enjoyed. But that enjoyment can be prolonged by several different kinds of conversation. We may all be engaged in standing together against the outer world—all those fools outside who write newspaper articles about us which reveal their ghastly ignorance of the real work, and propose schemes which look very fine on paper but which, as we well know, are impracticable. As long as that conversation lasts, the profession appears a very fine one and its achievements very remarkable; if only those yapping outsiders would leave us alone to get on with the job. And that conversation, if we could do it well enough, would make *one* kind of Kipling story. But we might equally spend the evening standing together against our own seniors: those people at the top—Lord knows how they got there while better men rot in provincial lectureships, or small ships, or starving parishes !—who seem to have forgotten what the real work is like and who spoil all our best efforts with their meddling and are quite deceived about our relative merits. And while that conversation lasted, our profession would appear a very rotten and heartbreaking profession. We might even say it was high time the public learned the sort of things that really go on. A rousing scandal might do good. And out of all that, *another* kind of Kipling story might be made. But then, some other evening, or later the same evening, we might all be standing together against our juniors. As if by magic our profession would now once more appear in a favourable light—at least, our profession as it used to be. What may happen with the sort of young cubs we're getting into it nowadays is another question. They need licking into shape. They'll have to learn to pull their socks up. They haven't begun to realise what is expected of them. And heaven knows, things are made easy enough for them now! They haven't been through the sort of mill we were through. God! If they'd worked under old So-and-so . . . and thus, yet *another* Kipling story might arise. But we sometimes like talking about our juniors in exactly the opposite way. We have been in the job so long that we have no illusions about it. We know that half the official regulations are dead letters. Nobody will thank you for doing more than you need. Our juniors are laughably full of zeal, pedantic about discipline, devoured with a morbid passion for work. Ah, well, they'll soon get over it!

Now the point is that the similarity between all these conversations is overwhelmingly more important than the differences. It may well be chance which launches the evening on one of them rather than another, for they all give the same sort of pleasure, and that is the kind of pleasure which the great majority of Kipling's works both express and communicate. I am tempted to describe it as the pleasure of freemasonry; but this would be confusing because Kipling became a Mason in the narrower and official sense. But in the wider sense you may say he was born a Mason. One of the stories that pleased his childhood was, significantly, about "lions who were all Freemasons" and in "confederacy against some wicked baboon". The pleasure of confederacy against wicked Baboons, or even of confederacy *simpliciter*, is the cardinal fact about the Kipling world. To belong, to be inside, to be in the know, to be snugly together against the outsiders—that is what really matters; it is almost an accident who are cast for the rôle of outsiders (wicked Baboons) on any given occasion. And no one before Kipling had fully celebrated the potency of that snugness—the esoteric comedies and tragedies the mutual understanding, the highly specialised smile, or shrug, or nod, or shake of the head, which passes between fellow-professionals; the exquisite pleasure of being approved, the un-assuaged mortification of being despised, within that charmed circle, compared with which public fame and infamy are a mere idle breath. What is the good of the papers hiding it "'andsome" if "you know the army knows"? What is the good of excuses accepted by government if "the men of one's own kind" hold one condemned?

And this is how the Simla stories really fit in. They are not very good—all Kipling's women have baritone voices—and at first sight they are not very mature work. But look again. "If you don't know about things Up Above," says Kipling, after recording one of Mrs. Hauksbee's most improbable exploits, "you won't understand how to fit in, and you will say it is impossible." In other words, at this stage of Kipling's career Simla society (to which, it may be supposed, his *entrée* was rather precarious) is itself a secret society, an inner ring, and the stories about it are for those who are "in the know". That the secrets in this case should be very shabby ones and the knowledge offered us very disillusioned knowledge, is an effect of the writer's youth. Young writers, and specially young writers already enchanted by the lure of the Inner Ring, like to exaggerate the cynicism and sophistication of the great world; it makes them feel less young. One sees how he must have enjoyed writing "Simla is a strange place . . . nor is any man who has not spent at least ten seasons there qualified to pass judgement!" That is the spirit of nearly all Kipling's work, though it was later applied to inner rings more interesting than Simla. There is something delicious about these early flights of esotericism. "In India," he says, "where everyone knows everyone else"; and again, "I have lived long enough in India to know that it is best to know nothing."

The great merit in Kipling is to have presented the magic of the Inner Ring in all its manifold workings for the first time. Earlier writers had presented it only in the form of snobbery; and snobbery is a very highly specialised form of it. The call of the Inner Ring, the men we know, the old firm, the talking of "shop", may call a man away from high society into very low society indeed; we desire not to be in a *junto* simply, just to be in that *junto* where we "belong". Nor is Kipling in the least mistaken when he attributes to this esoteric spirit such great powers for good. The professional point of honour (it means as much, said McPhee, as her virginity to a lassie), the *Aidôs* we feel only before our colleagues, the firm brotherhood of those who have "been through it" together, are things quite indispensable to the running of the world. This masonry or confederacy daily carries commonplace people to heights of diligence or courage which they would not be likely to reach by any private moral ideals. Without it, no good thing is operative widely or for long.

But also—and this Kipling never seems to notice—without it no bad thing is operative either. The nostalgia which sends the old soldier back to the army ("I smelt the smell of the barricks, I 'eard the bugles go") also sends the recidivist back to his old partner and his old "fence". The confidential glance or rebuke from a colleague is indeed the means whereby a weak brother is brought or kept up to the standard of a noble profession; it is also the means whereby a new and hitherto innocent member is initiated into the corruption of a bad one. "It's always done," they say; and so, without any "scenes" or excitement, with a nod and a wink, over a couple of whiskies and soda, the Rubicon is crossed. The spirit of the Inner Ring is morally neutral—the obedient servant of valour and public spirit, but equally of cruelty, extortion, oppression, and dishonesty.

Kipling seems unaware of this, or indifferent to it. He is the slave of the Inner Ring; he expresses the passion, but does not stand outside to criticise it. He plays for his side; about the choice of sides, about the limitations of partisanship after the side has been chosen, he has nothing very much to say to us. Mr. Eliot has, I think rightly, called him a Pagan. Irreverence is the last thing of which one could accuse him. He has a reverent Pagan agnosticism about all ultimates. "When a man has come to the turnstiles of Night," he says in the preface to *Life's Handicap*, "all the creeds in the world seem to him wonderfully alike and colourless." He has the Pagan tolerance too; a tolerance so wide (which is unusual) that it extends even to Christianity, whose phraseology he freely uses for rhetorical effect in his more Swinburnian moments.[1] But the tolerance is weary and sceptical; the whole energy of the man goes into his worship of the little demigods or daemons in the foreground—the Trades, the Sides, the Inner Rings. Their credentials he hardly examines. These servants he has made masters; these half-gods exclude the gods.

There are, I allow, hints of another Kipling. There are moments of an almost quivering tenderness—he himself had been badly hurt—when he writes of children or for them. And there are the "queer" or "rum" stories—*At the End of the Passage, The Mark of the Beast, They, Wireless*. These may be his best work, but they are not his most characteristic. If you open him at random, the chances are you will find him enslaved to some Inner Ring. His English countryside with its way of life is partly loved because

[1] Some poems could not, on internal evidence alone, be distinguished from Christian work.

American millionaires can't understand it, aren't in the know. His comic stories are nearly all about hoaxes: an outsider mystified is his favourite joke. His jungle is not free from it. His very railway engines are either recruits or Mulvaneys dressed up in boilers. His polo-ponies are public school ponies. Even his saints and angels are in a celestial civil service. It is this ubiquitous presence of the Ring, this unwearied knowingness, that renders his work in the long run suffocating and unendurable. And always, ironically, that bleak misgiving—almost that Nothingness—in the background.

But he was a very great writer. This trade-passion, this business of the Inner Ring, fills an immense area of human life. There, though not in the conventional novel, it frequently proves itself stronger than family affection, national loyalty, religion, and even vice. Hence Kipling's deserved success with thousands of readers who left older fiction to be read by women and boys. He came home to their bosoms by coming home to their business and showed them life as they had found it to be. This is merit of a high order; it is like the discovery of a new element or a new planet; it is, in its way and as far as it goes, a "return to nature". The remedy for what is partial and dangerous in his view of life is to go on from Kipling and to add the necessary correctives— not to deny what he has shown. After Kipling there is no excuse for the assumption that all the important things in a man's life happen between the end of one day's work and the beginning of the next. There is no good putting on airs about Kipling. The things he mistook for gods may have been only "spirits of another sort"; but they are real things and strong.

An Address to the English Association

5

Sir Walter Scott

HERE IN Edinburgh, on 7th June 1826, Walter Scott was kept awake nearly all night by a howling dog. He was in poor health. He was working at the highest pressure, convinced that such efforts might still recover his honour and perhaps even his fortune. His wife was barely three weeks dead. But he must not stop to think of that. He chides himself in his *Gurnal* for the "hysterical passion of terrible violence—a sort of throttling sensation" which impelled his solitary tears and was followed by "a state of dreaming stupidity" (30th May). For all depended on work; and work on health; and health on sleep. In such circumstances we can imagine what most men would have said about that howling dog; especially most literary men. One thinks of Carlyle. What Scott said will be familiar to many members of this society: "Poor cur! I dare say he had his distresses as I have mine." In those dozen words the whole sweetness and light of Scott's mind is revealed. I think I want to stress the light even more than the sweetness. We know from other evidence that few men have loved dogs more judiciously. As Lockhart's Mr. Adolphus delightfully says: "He was a gentleman even to his dogs." But that is hardly the point here. There is no parade of his love for animals. He flings to the poor cur a word of commiseration, but what is chiefly before his mind is indisputable fact; dogs don't howl at night if they are happy. There is here a clear-eyed recognition that there are in the world all sorts of creatures and that Scott with his distresses is only one of them. It is of a piece with his last recorded words, in answer to Lockhart's question whether he should send for Sophia and Anne: "No. Don't disturb them. I know they've been up all night." There is in both the same fidelity to common facts. Scott may be ruined, or bereaved, or dying; but dogs will howl and young women need sleep.

For the whole of that *Gurnal*, indeed, we might borrow a title from an author whom Scott himself fully appreciated, and call it "Sense and Sensibility". The sense, I presume, is obvious enough. We see it, first and foremost, in his cool and moderate estimate of his own literary powers; a modesty almost (one would have thought) impossible in one whose reputation had filled Europe and been blown up until he was put above Goethe and almost equalled with Shakespeare. Yet it is not mere self-depreciation. Though never deceived about his weaknesses, he knows his real strength too; the "hurried frankness of composition which pleases soldiers, sailors, and young people of bold and active disposition". He recognises, in his own way, the quality of what a more pretentious writer would call "inspiration":—"I shall get warm as I work"—the morning, fresh from the labours of subconscious artistry, is *musis amica*. We see it also in his unchanging, cheerfully unemphatic, contempt for "the imaginary consequence of literary triflers" and the "affectations of literature". We see it, this time co-operating with something even more precious than good sense, in his attitude to certain feelings which prey upon most of us at times; as when he notes (6th April 1826):

"I had the great pleasure to hear through a letter from Sir Adam, that Sophia was in health and Johnnie gaining strength. It is a fine exchange from deep and aching uncertainty . . . to the little spitfire feeling of *Well, but they might have taken the trouble to write.*"

Of all who have "little spitfire feelings", few, I believe, name them so honestly or so happily.

94

But we should do Scott little service with some modern critics by insisting exclusively on his sense; for there is a widespread opinion that genius is never free from neurosis, and unless we can find *Angst* in an author's soul he will hardly be taken seriously. Well, if we demand *Angst*, Scott can supply that, too. He confesses to "idle fears, gloomy thoughts" (11th April 1826); to "a thick throbbing at my heart . . . fancies thronging on me . . . a disposition to think on things melancholy and horrible" (24th October 1827). He notes repeatedly, and notes as irrational, a horror of "redding" his papers, so great that the task would leave him with "nerves shaking like a frightened child" (10th May 1829). He has known a day when there was "a vile sense of want of reality" in all he did and said. He was aware of some connection between these infirmities and the powers which made him an author. These sinkings of the imagination "come to a gifted, as it is called, but often unhappy class", who, as he unexpectedly adds, "but for the dictates of religion, or the natural recoil of the mind from the idea of dissolution", would often have been disposed to commit suicide (28th November 1826). All this, however, must be sought in the *Gurnal* and there alone. That, perhaps, is where Scott differs most from the type of artist dear to the modern psychological critic. The blue devils do not haunt his work; they leave no trail of laudanum, drink, divorce, tantrums, perversions, or paranoia across his life. As he says, "I generally affect good spirits in company of my family, whether I am enjoying them or not" (24th September 1827).

This is plainly a different thing from that "sincerity" which is often praised, and which might perhaps better be called incontinence. Yet the *Gurnal* is, I believe, one of the sincerest books in the world, and (which is not exactly the same thing) full of self-knowledge. How severely he exercised this sincerity may be gauged by the entry of 5th March 1826, where, finding something that savours a little of rhodomontade in the entry of the previous evening, he says, "I have sworn I will not blot out what I have once written here." I believe few of us would care to keep a diary under a strict rule against erasure. And to Scott such a rule would perhaps be more costly than to most men; Scott who rightly diagnosed pride as his ruling passion (5th February 1826), and who, when the pen dropped finally from his hand and irresistible tears from his eyes, said, "Friends, don't let me expose myself. Get me to bed" (Lockhart, X, p. 212).

The absence of the blue devils from his work, its freedom from all petulance, morbidity or shrillness, will not now, I am afraid, be regarded as wholly a virtue. Some will feel that, with the devils, much else, which ought to have come in, was excluded. We should certainly not guess from reading the Waverley Novels that their author had said in his diary, "Life could not be endured were it seen in reality" (21st December 1825); or again, "I have never yet found that ill-will dies in debt, or what is called gratitude distresses herself by frequent payments" (2nd March). Many moderns will think his maxim that "a melancholy catastrophe" or unhappy ending should "always be avoided" in fiction (28th July 1826), unsound and arbitrary in itself, and veritably disgraceful when we find it in conjunction with such dark estimates of life and men. This will seem to them, for all I have said about the sincerity of the man, to impute a fundamental dishonesty in the work.

But I think much can be said in answer to such a charge. In the first place, these tragic, or disillusioned passages in the *Gurnal* are only occasional, and spring very clearly from Scott's momentary situation. We are not called upon to believe, and I myself do not believe, that they represent Scott's settled criticism of life. And if they did, what then? Need we reject as worthless that gusto, that ease and good temper, that fine masculine cheerfulness, which is diffused over all the best of his novels and is perhaps

their greatest permanent attraction? If this could be shown to be
indeed inconsistent with Scott's most permanent conscious
thoughts, what should we have to say but that something in his
less conscious mind, something that brought his stories to him
while he slept, had taken over the pen and forced him to utter
the life he experienced rather than the life he saw when he
reflected. For, of course, something far more is involved than the
mere choice between happy and unhappy endings. Both can be
contrived, and both with good or bad motives. But the general
tone, the thing that makes, as it were, the smell or taste of the
whole book, cannot. In modern times we have been advised (and
on the whole, I think, rightly) always to trust the tone or impression of a man's work rather than his conscious and articulate
reflections, where the two disagree. The maxim is, of course,
most often applied by those who are finding concealed scepticism, prurience, or despair in authors professedly pious, edifying,
or optimistic. Perhaps we shall have to use it the other way round
for Scott, and say that the tapestry in Jonathan Oldbuck's spare
room, the language of Ochiltree, or the whole character of Baillie
Nichol Jarvie, convey to us a sense of life which is more important, more fully realised, than any mere "views" to the contrary
which Scott may be supposed to have held.

Secondly—and this is of more importance to literature—I think
any such criticism would involve trying Scott by laws which he
never acknowledged. It is now very generally demanded that a
novel should be "a comment on life". Unless the meaning of this
phrase is attenuated almost to nonentity, I do not think Scott
supposed a novel to be anything of the sort. As Lord David Cecil
has pointed out, the English novel descends from the English
comedy. Not, of course, from English farce, nor necessarily from
the comedy of intrigue; we must include under our definition of
comedy things like *The Merchant of Venice* and *Twelfth Night*.
The purpose of the older novel, as of such pieces, was not to

comment on life. I do not think that was the primary purpose
of the tragedies either, nor of such novels as ended tragically.
I do not think tragedy and comedy differed by expressing
different views of life. The difference was more that between
Forms. Both were deliberate patterns or arrangements of possible
(but by no means necessarily probable) events chosen for their
harmonious unity in variety, deliberately modified, contrasted,
balanced in a fashion which real life never permits. Different
degrees of verisimilitude occur in different pieces, but I think the
verisimilitude is always a means, not an end. Improbability is
avoided, when at all, not because the author wants to tell us what
life is like, but because he fears lest too gross an improbability
should make the audience incredulous and therefore unreceptive
of the mood or passion he is trying to evoke. I think this was
Scott's attitude. He usually rejected unhappy endings not because
he believed, or wanted his readers to believe, or even for a
moment supposed they would believe, that irretrievable dis-
asters never occurred in real life, but because they were inconsistent with the sort of work he was making and would not
contribute to its οἰκεία ἡδονή. He was not (save very incidentally)
saying something about the world but making an *objet d'art* of a
particular kind. If you like you may, no doubt, say that he was
an entertainer; if you must, I suppose no one can prevent your
saying "a mere entertainer". That is, his work belongs with the
Decameron, The Canterbury Tales, the *Furioso* (one of his own
great favourites), *The Marriage of Figaro, Pickwick,* and *The Moon-
stone;* not with *The Divine Comedy, War and Peace,* or *The Ring.*

The distinction I am making is sometimes expressed by using
the word *serious* of the works which fall in my second class. But
I think the adjective unhappy because it is ambiguous. In one
sense (and this I think is the most useful sense for critics) *serious*
is simply the opposite of *comic.* In that sense, of course, Tupper
and Patience Strong are serious artists, and Aristophanes is not.

But *serious* may mean "worthy of serious consideration". In that sense a gay song by Prior may be more *serious* than some of the most lugubrious items in our hymn-books. What is more, a pure *divertissement* may be more *serious* than a long, well-documented tendentious, ethical, or sociological novel: *Guy Mannering* more *serious* than *Mr. Britling Sees It Through*.

There remains, however, a third sense in which Scott can be accused of insufficient seriousness. This has nothing to do with the *genre* he was writing. The *Furioso* is a light work, but Ariosto did not take it lightly; witness those famous variations in the first line. But Scott often took his work very lightly indeed. There is little sign, even in his best days, of a serious and costly determination to make each novel as good in its own kind as he could make it. And at the end, when he is writing to pay off his debts, his attitude to his own work is, by some standards, scandalous and cynical. Anything will do, provided it will sell. He says of *Castle Dangerous* and *Count Robert of Paris*, "I think the public are mad for passing those two volumes; but I will not be the first to cry them down" (26th January 1832).

Here we come to an irreducible opposition between Scott's outlook and that of our more influential modern men of letters. These would blame him for disobeying his artistic conscience; Scott would have said he was obeying his conscience. He knew only one kind of conscience. It told him that a man must pay his debts if he possibly could. The idea that some supposed obligation to write good novels could override this plain, universal demand of honesty, would have seemed to him the most pitiful subterfuge of vanity and idleness, and a prime specimen of that "literary sensibility" or "affected singularity" which he most heartily despised.

Two different worlds here clash. And who am I to judge between them? It may be true, as Curtius has said, that "the modern world immeasurably overvalues art". Or it may be that the modern world is right and that all previous ages have greatly erred in making art, as they did, subordinate to life, so that artists worked to teach virtue, to adorn the city, to solemnise feasts and marriages, to please a patron, or to amuse the people. Or again, a middle view may be possible; that works of art are in reality serious, and ends in themselves, but that all is lost when the artists discover this, as Eros fled when Psyche turned the lamp upon him. But wherever the truth may lie, there are two things of which I feel certain. One is, that if we do overvalue art, then art itself will be the greatest sufferer; when second things are put first, they are corrupted. The other is that, even if we of all generations have first valued art aright, yet there will certainly be loss as well as gain. We shall lose the fine careless, prodigal artists. For, if not all art, yet some art, flows best from men who treat their work as a kind of play. I at any rate cannot conceive how the exuberance, the elbow-room, the heart-easing quality of Dickens, or Chaucer, or Cervantes, could co-exist with that self-probing literary conscience we find in Pater or Henry James. Lockhart speaks somewhere of Scott "enjoying rather than exerting his genius". We may be coming to a period when there will be no room for authors who do that. If so, I admit there may be gains; I am sure there will be losses.

This leads me naturally to the question of Scott's style. One is sometimes tempted to say that the veriest journeyman among us could mend a thousand passages in the novels. Nothing could easily be worse than the sentence in which Mannering looks up and the planets "rolled" above him, "each in its orbit of liquid light". This, perhaps, is exceptional; what is unfortunately constant is the polysyllabic, uneconomical, even florid, texture of his narrative and descriptive writing. His dialogue, of course, is a wholly different thing. Let but Andrew Fairservice, or the Baillie, or douce Davie Deans, or Jonathan Oldbuck, or even Julia Mannering open their mouths, and at once we have race and piquancy, the living and the concrete. Most interestingly, in the *Gurnal*, we find Scott using in his own person both the style that repels and that which conquers us.

Thus he refers to the news of his wife's death as "the melancholy intelligence" (15th May 1826). What a choke-pear! And what a use of the word *melancholy*, how calculated to spoil it for contexts where it is really needed! Nor must we plead that Lady Scott was not, after all, the great passion of her husband's life. That, I think, is true; but the phrase is still far too vague and ready-made for the deep affliction which her death was to him. He himself puts that beyond doubt by the words with which, next day, he expresses its precise nature and degree: "I wonder how I shall do with the large portion of thoughts which were hers for thirty years" (16th May 1826). I think the experience of all bereavements, the daily and hourly setting out of the thoughts upon a familiar road, forgetful of the grim frontier-post that now blocks it, the repeated frustration which renews not only sorrow but the surprise of sorrow, has seldom been more truthfully conveyed.

Here is another example. On 18th December 1825 he is facing the thought that Abbotsford may have to be sold. He writes, "The recollection of the extensive woods I planted, and the walks I have formed, from which strangers must derive both the pleasure and the profit, will excite feelings likely to sober my gayest moments... My dogs will wait for me in vain." This is, of course, better writing than "the melancholy intelligence". But the vocabulary is curiously dead. Then comes a space in the MS.; then the unconscious master-stroke—"I find my dogs' feet on my knees".

And this happens again and again in the *Gurnal*. We find side by side that style which Scott habitually used for narrative and another style, far more sensitive, which, if he had more often employed it, would have given him a far higher literary place than he actually holds. In the novels this better style hardly appears except in dialogue and (especially) in dialect. As a stylist Wandering Willie can play his creator off the field; he has more music in his sporran than the Sheriff in his whole body; and Julia Mannering, at her best, more wit.

For his public, and inferior, style reasons can be found, one local, the other historical. It was Professor Nichol Smith who first pointed out to me that a love of the polysyllable had been endemic in Scotland ever since the time of Henryson. He said that in this very city he himself had attended, in youth, a debating society where students were always rising "to homologate the sentiments of the previous speaker". But in Scott's time this local and national infirmity was only the aggravation of a disease which then held the whole island in its grip. We must not allow a few great and highly idiosyncratic writers like Lamb, Hazlitt, and Landor, to blind us to the fact that the early nineteenth century found English in a bloated condition. The abstract is preferred to the concrete. The word farthest from the soil is liked best; we find *personage* or *individual* for *man*, *female* for *woman*, *monarch* for *king*. Hence Wordsworth, even in poetry, will have his *itinerant vehicle, female vagrant,* and *casual refreshment*. Scott, I am afraid, nearly always called food *refreshment*, and is among those who have helped to spoil that potentially beautiful word for ever.

Stylistically, then, Scott lived in an unfortunate period, and his real strength was allowed to come out only in dialogue. This, I think, must be conceded. But let us not concede too much. Even his narrative style has the qualities of its defects. The cheerful rattle of his polysyllables (often energetic in rhythm even where flaccid in syntax and vocabulary), the very sense that not much care is being taken, and the brisk, virile pace, all help us to feel that we are off on a journey of pleasure. The jingle of the harness creates the holiday mood; and "with tolerable horses and a civil driver" (as Scott promises in *Waverley*, V) we jog along, on the whole, very contentedly.

But whatever may be said against Scott's style or his contrived (and often ill-contrived) plots it will not touch the essential glory of the Waverley Novels. That glory is in my opinion, twofold.

First, these novels almost created that historical sense which we now all take for granted, and by which we often condemn Scott himself. Of course, he makes historical blunders and even treasures historical illusions. But he, first of men, taught us the feeling for period. Chaucer's Trojans are medieval people. Shakespeare's Romans are Elizabethan people. The characters in *Otranto* are so patently Walpole's contemporaries that no one could now believe in them. Scott everywhere—insufficiently, no doubt, but he was a pioneer—reminds us that our ancestors were different from ourselves. I have high authority for my statement. It was the Master of Trinity, Professor Trevelyan, who first pointed out to me the difference in this respect between the *Decline and Fall* and Macaulay's *History*. Gibbon, he said, writes as if every Roman emperor, every Gothic chieftain, and every hermit in the Thebaid, was an eighteenth century man. But Macaulay is always pressing upon us the difference between his own age and the age he depicts. "And I attribute this almost wholly," said the Master, "to the fact that the Waverley Novels had come in between." Once it had been said, it seemed to me obvious. And if it is, then to concentrate on Scott's errors in history is like trying to make Columbus unimportant because he failed to produce a full map of America. Scott, like Columbus, is among the great discoverers. If we are now so conscious of period, that we feel more difference between decades than our ancestors felt between centuries, we owe this, for good or ill, to Scott.

Secondly, the novels embody these immensely valuable qualities of mind which I have claimed for the *Gurnal*. They may lack many virtues which the novel has achieved since; but they have those virtues of which no age is in more desperate need than our own. They have their own essential rectitude. They slur some things; they exaggerate nothing. Minor frailties are never worked up into enormous sins, nor petty distresses into factitious tragedies. Everything is in proportion. Consider what either Dickens on the one hand, or George Moore on the other, would have made of Effie Deans. Then turn back to Scott and breathe the air of sense.

But I must come to an end. You may feel that I have spent too much time on this great author's faults and too little on his excellences. But that is because I am speaking among his friends. Where else does one mention the faults of a man one loves? And Scott today has few friends. Our juniors are ill at ease in his presence. One of these has said that Scott wholly misunderstood his own story in *The Heart of Midlothian*, for the tale makes it quite clear that the heroine's real motive for refusing to commit perjury "must have been" unconscious jealousy of her sister's beauty. It is like reading a review by a jackal on a book written by a lion. But we must not grow bitter. Perhaps we shall some day climb out of this present trough; as Scott delighted to quote, "Patience, cousin, and shuffle the cards." And even if no change ever comes, if the barbarism on which we now seem to be entering is to prove the last illness, the death-bed of humanity, we must not rail at those who are its victims. Let us only say, adapting Scott's own words, "Poor curs. I dare say they have their distresses." And indeed they have.

A Toast proposed to the Edinburgh Sir Walter Scott Club, 1956

6

Lilies that Fester

IN THE "Cambridge Number" of the *Twentieth Century* (1955) Mr. John Allen asked why so many people "go to such lengths to prove to us that really they are not intellectuals at all and certainly not cultured". I believe I know the answer. Two parallels may help to ease it into the reader's mind.

We all know those who shudder at the word *refinement* as a term of social approval. Sometimes they express their dislike of this usage by facetiously spelling it *refanement*, with the implication that it is likely to be commonest in the mouths of those whose speech has a certain varnished vulgarity. And I suppose we can all understand the shudder, whether we approve it or not. He who shudders feels that the quality of mind and behaviour which we call *refined* is nowhere less likely to occur than among those who aim at, and talk much about, *refinement*. Those who have this quality are not obeying any idea of *refinement* when they abstain from swaggering, spitting, snatching, triumphing, calling names, boasting or contradicting. These modes of behaviour do not occur to them as possibles: if they did, that training and sensibility which constitute refinement would reject them as disagreeables, without reference to any ideal of conduct, just as we reject a bad egg without reference to its possible effect on our stomachs. *Refinement*, in fact, is a name given to certain behaviour from without. From within, it does not appear as *refinement*; indeed, it does not appear, does not become an object of consciousness, at all. Where it is most named it is most absent.

I produce my next parallel with many different kinds of reluctance. But I think it too illuminating to be omitted. The word *religion* is extremely rare in the New Testament or the writings of mystics. The reason is simple. Those attitudes and practices to which we give the collective name of *religion* are themselves concerned with religion hardly at all. To be religious is to have one's attention fixed on God and on one's neighbour in relation to God. Therefore, almost by definition, a religious man, or a man when he is being religious, is not thinking about *religion*; he hasn't the time. *Religion* is what we (or he himself at a later moment) call his activity from outside.

Of course those who disdain the words *refinement* and *religion* may be doing so from bad motives; they may wish to impress us with the idea that they are well-bred or holy. Such people are regarding chatter about *refinement* or *religion* simply as symptomatic of vulgarity or worldliness, and eschew the symptom to clear themselves from the suspicion of the disease. But there are others who sincerely and (I believe) rightly think that such talk is not merely a symptom of, but a cause active in producing, that disease. The talk is inimical to the thing talked of, likely to spoil it where it exists and to prevent its birth where it is unborn.

Now *culture* seems to belong to the same class of dangerous and embarrassing words. Whatever else it may mean, it certainly covers deep and genuine enjoyment of literature and the other arts. (By using the word *enjoyment* I do not mean to beg the vexed question about the rôle of pleasure in our experience of the arts. I mean *frui*, not *delectari*; as we speak of a man "enjoying" good health or an estate.) Now if I am certain of anything in the world, I am certain that while a man is, in this sense, enjoying *Don Giovanni* or the *Oresteia* he is not caring one farthing about *culture*. Culture? the irrelevance of it! For just as to be fat or clever means to be fatter or cleverer than most, so to be *cultured* must mean to be more so than most, and thus the very word carries the mind at once to comparisons, and groupings, and life in society. And what has all that to do with the horns that blow as the statue enters, or Clytæmnestra crying, "Now you have named me aright ?" In *Howard's End* Mr. E. M. Forster excellently describes a girl listening to a symphony. She is not thinking about *culture*: nor about "Music"; nor even about "this music". She sees the whole world through the music. *Culture*, like religion, is a name given from outside to activities which are not themselves interested in *culture* at all, and would be ruined the moment they were.

I do not mean that we are never to talk of things from the outside. But when the things are of high value and very easily destroyed, we must talk with great care, and perhaps the less we talk the better. To be constantly engaged with the idea of *culture*, and (above all) of *culture* as something enviable, or meritorious, or something that confers prestige, seems to me to endanger those very "enjoyments" for whose sake we chiefly value it. If we encourage others, or ourselves, to hear, see, or read great art on the ground that it is a *cultured* thing to do, we call into play precisely those elements in us which must be in abeyance before we can enjoy art at all. We are calling up the desire for self-improvement, the desire for distinction, the desire to revolt (from one group) and to agree (with another), and a dozen busy passions which, whether good or bad in themselves, are, in relation to the arts, simply a blinding and paralysing distraction.

At this point some may protest that by *culture* they do not mean the "enjoyments" themselves, but the whole habit of mind which such experiences, reacting upon one another, and reflected on, build up as a permanent possession. And some will wish to include the sensitive and enriching social life which, they think, will arise among groups of people who share this habit of mind. But this reinterpretation leaves me with the same difficulty. I can well imagine a lifetime of such enjoyments leading a man to such a habit of mind, but on one condition; namely, that he went to the arts for no such purpose. Those who read poetry to improve their minds will never improve their minds by reading poetry. For the true enjoyments must be spontaneous and compulsive and look to no remoter end. The Muses will submit to no marriage of convenience. The desirable habit of mind, if it is to come at all, must come as a by-product, unsought. The idea of making it one's aim suggests that shattering confidence which Goethe made to Eckermann: "In all my youthful amours the object I had in view was my own ennoblement." To this, I presume, most of us would reply that, even if we believe a love-affair can ennoble a young man, we feel sure that a love-affair undertaken for that purpose would fail of its object. Because of course it wouldn't be a love-affair at all.

So much for the individual. But the claims made for the "cultured" group raise an embarrassing question. What, exactly, is the evidence that *culture* produces among those who share it a sensitive and enriching social life? If by "sensitive" we mean "sensitive to real or imagined affronts", a case could be made out. Horace noted long ago that "bards are a touchy lot". The lives and writings of the Renaissance Humanists and the correspondence in the most esteemed literary periodicals of our own century will show that critics and scholars are the same. But *sensitive* in that meaning cannot be combined with *enriching*. Competitive and resentful egoisms can only impoverish social life. The sensitivity that enriches must be of the sort that guards a man from wounding others, not of the sort that makes him ready to feel wounded himself. Between this sensitivity and *culture*, my own experience does not suggest any causal connection. I have often found it among the uncultured. Among the cultured I have sometimes found it and sometimes not.

Let us be honest. I claim to be one of the cultured myself and have no wish to foul my own nest. Even if that claim is disallowed, I have at least lived among them and would not denigrate my friends. But we are speaking here among ourselves—behind closed doors. Frankness is best. The real traitor to our order is not the man who speaks, within that order, of its faults, but the man who flatters our corporate self-complacency. I gladly admit that we number among us men and women whose modesty, courtesy, fair-mindedness, patience in disputation and readiness to see an antagonist's point of view, are wholly admirable. I am fortunate to have known them. But we must also admit that we show as high a percentage as any group whatever of bullies, paranoiacs, and poltroons, of backbiters, exhibitionists, mopes, milksops, and world-without-end bores. The loutishness that turns every argument into a quarrel is really no rarer among us than among the sub-literate; the restless inferiority-complex ("stern to inflict" but not "stubborn to endure") which bleeds at a touch but scratches like a wildcat is almost as common among us as among schoolgirls.

If you doubt this, try an experiment. Take any one of those who vaunt most highly the adjusting, cleansing, liberating, and civilising effects of *culture* and ask him about other poets, other critics, other scholars, not in the mass but one by one and name by name. Nine times out of ten he will deny of each what he claimed for all. He will certainly produce very few cases in which, on his own showing, *culture* has had its boasted results. Sometimes we suspect that he can think of only one. The conclusion most naturally to be drawn from his remarks is that the praise our order can most securely claim is that which Dr. Johnson gave to the Irish. "They are an honest people; they never speak well of one another."

It is then (at best) extremely doubtful whether *culture* produces any of those qualities which will enable people to associate with one another graciously, loyally, understandingly, and with permanent delight. When Ovid said that it "softened our manners", he was flattering a barbarian king. But even if *culture* did all these things, we could not embrace it for their sake. This would be to use consciously and self-consciously, as means to extraneous ends, things which must lose all their power of conducing to those ends by the very fact of being so used. For many modern exponents of *culture* seem to me to be "impudent" in the etymological sense; they lack *pudor,* they have no shyness where men ought to be shy. They handle the most precious and fragile things with the roughness of an auctioneer and talk of our most intensely solitary and fugitive experiences as if they were selling us a Hoover. It is all really very well summed up in Mr. Allen's phrase in the *Twentieth Century* "the faith in culture". A "faith in culture" is as bad as a faith in religion; both expressions imply a turning away from those very things which culture and religion are about. "Culture" as a collective name for certain very valuable activities is a permissible word; but *culture* hypostatised, set up on its own, made into a faith, a cause, a banner, a "platform", is unendurable. For none of the activities in question cares a straw for that faith or cause. It is like a return to early Semitic religion where names themselves were regarded as powers.

Now a step further. Mr. Allen complained that, not content with creeping out of earshot when we can bear the voices of certain *culture*-mongers no longer, we then wantonly consort, or pretend that we consort, with the lowest of the low-brows, and affect to share their pleasures. There are at this point a good many allusions which go over my head. I don't know what A F N is, I am not fond of cellars, and modern whisky suits neither my purse, my palate, nor my digestion. But I think I know the sort of thing he has in mind, and I think I can account for it. As before, I will begin with a parallel. Suppose you had spent an evening among very young and very transparent snobs who were feigning a discriminating enjoyment of a great port, though anyone who knew could see very well that, if they had ever drunk port in their lives before, it came from a grocer's. And then suppose that on your journey home you went into a grubby little tea-shop and there heard an old body in a feather boa say to another old body, with a smack of her lips, "That was a nice cup o' tea, dearie, that was. Did me good." Would you not, at that moment, feel that this was like fresh mountain air? For here, at last, would be something real. Here would be a mind really concerned about that in which it expressed concern. Here would be pleasure, here would be undebauched experience, spontaneous and compulsive, from the fountain-head. A live dog is better than a dead lion. In the same way, after a certain kind of sherry party, where there have been cataracts of *culture* but never one word or one glance that suggested a real enjoyment of any art, any person, or any natural object, my heart warms to the schoolboy on the bus who is reading *Fantasy and Science Fiction*, rapt and oblivious of all the world beside. For here also I should feel that I had met something real and live and unfabricated; genuine literary experience, spontaneous and compulsive, disinterested. I should have hopes of that boy. Those who have greatly cared for any book whatever may possibly come to care, some day, for good books. The organs of appreciation exist in them. They are not impotent. And even if this particular boy is never going to like anything severer than science-fiction, even so,

> The child whose love is here, at least doth reap
> One precious gain, that he forgets himself.

I should still prefer the live dog to the dead lion; perhaps, even, the wild dog to the over-tame poodle or Peke.

I should not have spent so many words on answering Mr. Allen's question (neither of us matters sufficiently to justify it) unless I thought that the discussion led to something of more consequence. This I will now try to develop. Mr. Forster feels anxious because he dreads Theocracy. Now if he expects to see a Theocracy set up in modern England, I myself believe his expectation to be wholly chimerical. But I wish to make it very clear that, if I thought the thing in the least probable, I should feel about it exactly as he does. I fully embrace the maxim (which he borrows from a Christian) that "all power corrupts". I would go further. The loftier the pretensions of the power, the more meddlesome, inhuman, and oppressive it will be. Theocracy is the worst of all possible governments. All political power is at best a necessary evil: but it is least evil when its sanctions are most modest and commonplace, when it claims no more than to be useful or convenient and sets itself strictly limited objectives. Anything transcendental or spiritual, or even anything very strongly ethical, in its pretensions is dangerous and encourages it to meddle with our private lives. Let the shoemaker stick to his last. Thus the Renaissance doctrine of Divine Right is for me a corruption of monarchy; Rousseau's General Will, of democracy; racial mysticisms, of nationality. And Theocracy, I admit and even insist, is the worst corruption of all. But then I don't think we are in any danger of it. What I think we are really in danger of is something that would be only one degree less intolerable, and intolerable in almost the same way. I would call it Charientocracy; not the rule of the saints but the rule of the χαρίεντες, the *venustiores*, the Hotel de Rambouillet, the Wits, the Polite, the "Souls", the "Apostles", the Sensitive, the *Cultured*, the Integrated, or whatever the latest password may be. I will explain how I think it could come about.

The old social classes have broken up. Two results follow. On the one hand, since most men, as Aristotle observed, do not like to be merely equal with all other men, we find all sorts of people building themselves into groups within which they can feel superior to the mass; little unofficial, self-appointed aristocracies.

The *Cultured* increasingly form such a group. Notice their tendency to use the social term *vulgar* of those who disagree with them. Notice that Mr. Allen spoke of rebels against, or deserters from this group, as denying not that they are "intellectual" but that they are "intellectuals", not hiding a quality but deprecating inclusion in a class. On the other hand, inevitably, there is coming into existence a new, real, ruling class: what has been called the Managerial Class. The coalescence of these two groups, the unofficial, self-appointed aristocracy of the *Cultured* and the actual Managerial rulers, will bring us to Charientocracy.

But the two groups are already coalescing, because education is increasingly the means of access to the Managerial Class. And of course education, in some sense, is a very proper means of access; we do not want our rulers to be dunces. But education is coming to have a new significance. It aspires to do, and can do, far more to the pupil than education (except, perhaps, that of the Jesuits) has ever done before.

For one thing, the pupil is now far more defenceless in the hands of his teachers. He comes increasingly from businessmen's flats or workmen's cottages in which there are few books or none. He has hardly ever been alone. The educational machine seizes him very early and organises his whole life, to the exclusion of all unsuperintended solitude or leisure. The hours of unsponsored, uninspected, perhaps even forbidden, reading, the ramblings, and the "long, long thoughts" in which those of luckier generations first discovered literature and nature and themselves are a thing of the past. If a Traherne or a Wordsworth were born today he would be "cured" before he was twelve. In short, the modern pupil is the ideal patient for those masters who, not content with teaching a subject, would create a character; helpless Plasticine. Or if by chance (for nature will be nature) he should have any powers of resistance, they know how to deal with him. I am coming to that point in a moment.

H   113

Secondly, the nature of the teaching has changed. In a sense it had changed for the better: that is, it demands far more of the master and, in recompense, makes his work more interesting. It has become far more intimate and penetrating; more inward. Not content with making sure that the pupil has read and remembered the text, it aspires to teach him appreciation. It seems harsh to quarrel with what at first sounds so reasonable an aim. Yet there is a danger in it. Everyone now laughs at the old test-paper with its context questions and the like, and people ask, "What good can that sort of thing do a boy?" But surely to demand that the test-paper should do the boy good is like demanding that a thermometer should heat a room. It was the reading of the text which was supposed to do the boy good; you set the paper to find out if he had read it. And just because the paper did not force the boy to produce, or to feign, appreciation, it left him free to develop in private, spontaneously, as an out-of-school activity which would never earn any marks, such appreciation as he could. That was a private affair between himself and Virgil or himself and Shakespeare. Nine times out of ten, probably, nothing happened at all. But wherever appreciation did occur (and quite certainly it sometimes did) it was genuine; suited to the boy's age and character; no exotic, but the healthy growth of its native soil and weather. But when we substitute exercises in "practical criticism" for the old, dry papers, a new situation arises. The boy will not get good marks (which means, in the long run, that he will not get into the Managerial Class) unless he produces the kind of responses, and the kind of analytic method, which commend themselves to his teacher. This means at best that he is trained to the precocious anticipation of responses, and of a method, inappropriate to his years. At worst it means that he is trained in the (not very difficult) art of simulating the orthodox responses. For nearly all boys are good mimics. Depend upon it, before you have been teaching for a term, everyone in the form knows pretty well "the sort of stuff that goes down with Prickly Pop-eye". In the old days also they knew that what "went down", but the only thing that "went down" was correct answers to factual questions, and there were only two ways of producing those: working or cheating.

The thing would not be so bad if the responses which the pupils had to make were even those of the individual master. But we have already passed that stage. Somewhere (I have not yet tracked it down) there must be a kind of *culture*-mongers' central bureau which keeps a sharp look-out for deviationists. At least there is certainly someone who sends little leaflets to schoolmasters printing half a dozen poems on each and telling the master not only which the pupils must be made to prefer, but exactly on what grounds. (The impertinence of it! We know what Mulcaster or Boyer would have done with those leaflets.)

Thus to say that, under the nascent régime, education alone will get you into the ruling class, may not mean simply that the failure to acquire certain knowledge and to reach a certain level of intellectual competence will exclude you. That would be reasonable enough. But it may come to mean, perhaps means already, something more. It means that you cannot get in without becoming, or without making your masters believe that you have become, a very specific kind of person, one who makes the right responses to the right authors. In fact, you can get in only by becoming, in the modern sense of the word, *cultured*. This situation must be distinguished from one that has often occurred before. Nearly all ruling classes, sooner or later, in some degree or other, have taken up *culture* and patronised the arts. But when that happens the *culture* is the result of their position; one of the luxuries or privileges of their order. The situation we are now facing will be almost the opposite. Entry into the ruling class will be the reward of *culture*. Thus we reach Charientocracy.

Not only is the thing likely to happen; it is already planned and avowed. Mr. J. W. Saunders has set it all out in an excellent article entitled "Poetry in the Managerial Age" (*Essays in Criticism*, iv, 3, July 1954). He there faces the fact that modern poets are read almost exclusively by one another. He looks about for a remedy. Naturally he does not suggest that the poets should do anything about it. For it is taken as basic by all the *culture* of our age that whenever artists and audience lose touch, the fault must be wholly on the side of the audience. (I have never come across the great work in which this important doctrine is proved.) The remedy which occurs to Mr. Saunders is that we should provide our poets with a conscript audience; a privilege last enjoyed, I believe, by Nero. And he tells us how this can be done. We get our "co-ordinators" through education; success in examinations is the road into the ruling class. All that we need do, therefore, is to make not just poetry, but "the intellectual discipline which the critical reading of poetry can foster", the backbone of our educational system. In other words, practical criticism or something of the sort, exercised, no doubt, chiefly on modern poets, is to be the indispensable subject, failure in which excludes you from the Managerial Class. And so our poets get their conscript readers. Every boy or girl who is born is presented with the choice: "Read the poets whom we, the *cultured*, approve, and say the sort of things we say about them, or be a prole." And this (picking up a previous point) shows how Charientocracy can deal with the minority of pupils who have tastes of their own and are not pure Plasticine. They get low marks. You kick them off the educational ladder at a low rung and they disappear into the proletariat.

Another advantage is that, besides providing poets with a conscript audience for the moment, you can make sure that the regnant literary dynasty will reign almost for ever. For the deviationists whom you have kicked off the ladder will of course include all those troublesome types who, in earlier ages, were apt to start new schools and movements. If there had been a sound Charientocracy in their day, the young Chaucer, the young Donne, the young Wordsworth and Coleridge, could have been dealt with. And thus literary history, as we have known it in the past, may come to an end. Literary man, so long a wild animal, will have become a tame one.

Having explained why I think a Charientocracy probable, I must conclude by explaining why I think it undesirable.

Culture is a bad qualification for a ruling class because it does not qualify men to rule. The things we really need in our rulers— mercy, financial integrity, practical intelligence, hard work, and the like—are no more likely to be found in cultured persons than in anyone else.

Culture is a bad qualification in the same way as sanctity. Both are hard to diagnose and easy to feign. Of course not every charientocrat will be a cultural hypocrite nor every theocrat a Tartuffe. But both systems encourage hypocrisy and make the disinterested pursuit of the quality they profess to value more difficult.

But hypocrisy is not the only evil they encourage. There are, as in piety, so in *culture*, states which, if less culpable, are no less disastrous. In the one we have the "Goody-goody"; the docile youth who has neither revolted against nor risen above the routine pietisms and respectabilities of his home. His conformity has won the approval of his parents, his influential neighbours, and his own conscience. He does not know that he has missed anything and is content. In the other, we have the adaptable youth to whom poetry has always been something "Set" for "evaluation". Success in this exercise has given him pleasure and let him into the ruling class. He does not know what he has missed, does not know that poetry ever had any other purpose, and is content.

Both types are much to be pitied: but both can sometimes be very nasty. Both may exhibit spiritual pride, but each in its proper form, since the one has succeeded by acquiescence and repression, but the other by repeated victory in competitive performances. To the pride of the one, sly, simpering, and demure, we might apply Mr. Allen's word "smug" (especially if we let in a little of its older sense). My epithet for the other would, I think, be "swaggering". It tends in my experience to be raw, truculent, eager to give pain, insatiable in its demands for submission, resentful and suspicious of disagreement. Where the goody-goody slinks and sidles and purrs (and sometimes scratches) like a cat, his opposite number in the ranks of the *cultured* gobbles like an enraged turkey. And perhaps both types are less curable than the hypocrite proper. A hypocrite might (conceivably) repent and mend; or he might be unmasked and rendered innocuous. But who could bring to repentance, and who can unmask, those who were attempting no deception? who don't know that they are not the real thing because they don't know that there ever was a real thing?

Lastly I reach the point where my objections to Theocracy and to Charientocracy are almost identical. "Lilies that fester smell far worse than weeds." The higher the pretensions of our rulers are, the more meddlesome and impertinent their rule is likely to be and the more the thing in whose name they rule will be defiled. The highest things have the most precarious foothold in our nature. By making sanctity or culture a *moyen de parvenir* you help to drive them out of the world. Let our masters leave these two, at least, alone; leave us some region where the spontaneous, the unmarketable, the utterly private, can still exist.

As far as I am concerned, Mr. Allen fell short of the mark when he spoke of a "retreat from the faith in culture". I don't want retreat; I want attack or, if you prefer the word, rebellion. I write in the hope of rousing others to rebel. So far as I can see, the question has nothing to do with the difference between Christians and those who (unfortunately, since the word has long

Lilies that Fester

borne a useful, and wholly different, meaning) have been called "humanists". I hope that red herring will not be brought in. I would gladly believe that many atheists and agnostics care for the things I care for. It is for them I have written. To them I say: the "faith in culture" is going to strangle all those things unless we can strangle it first. And there is no time to spare.

Twentieth Century, 1955

7

Psycho-analysis and Literary Criticism

THE PURPOSE of this paper is by no means to attack psycho-analysis, but only to contribute to the solution of some frontier problems between psycho-analysis and literary criticism. One of these I consider a pseudo-problem. I am referring to the use which some critics make of psycho-analysis to infer the pathology of a poet from his work. When this is all that is done, and when it is made quite clear that the result is intended as a contribution not to literary criticism but to pathology, or pathological biography, I have, of course, nothing, good or bad, to say to it. Unfortunately, however, we sometimes meet with a real confusion in which the proposition "This poem is an inevitable outcome, and an illuminating symptom, of the poet's repressions" is somehow treated as an answer to the proposition "This poem is rubbish". The critic has allowed himself to be diverted from the genuinely critical question "Why, and how, should we read this?" to the purely historical question "Why did he write it?"—and that, too, in a sense which makes the word "why" mean not "with what intention?" but "impelled by what causes?" He is asking not for the Final Cause, which would still have some literary importance, but for the Efficient, which has none. With misunderstandings of this kind we need not concern ourselves.

I am going to deal with two Freudian positions, of which one will be found in the twenty-third of the *Introductory Lectures*.[1] At

[1] Freud, *Introductory Lectures*: translated by Joan Riviere (Allen and Unwin. London, 4th impression 1933), pp. 314, 315.

the end of that lecture all art is traced to the fantasies—that is the day-dreams or waking wish-fulfilments—of the artist. The artist wants "honour, power, riches, fame and the love of women", but being unable to get these in the real world, he has to do the best he can by imagining or pretending that he has got them. So far, according to Freud, he does not differ from the rest of us. What makes him an artist is the curious faculty he possesses of "elaborating his day-dreams so that they lose that personal note which grates upon strange ears, and become enjoyable to others". As we others also like a good wish-fulfilment dream, we are now ready to pay for the privilege of sharing his. Thus, for the artist, as Freud says, there is a path through fantasy back to reality: by publishing his mere dreams of "honour, power, riches, fame, and the love of women" he acquires "honour, power, riches, fame, and the love of women" in reality.

You will notice that this is a theory about readers as well as about writers. If Freud had been content to say that all works of art could be causally traced to Fantasy in the artist, he would be merely stating an efficient cause which we might find difficult to disprove. But he makes it clear that we enjoy the product as a fantasy—that reading, as well as writing, is wish fulfilment. Indeed it is obvious that be believes all imagining or day-dreaming to be of a single kind—that kind in which the dreamer pretends that he is a famous man, or a millionaire, or an irresistible lady-killer, while in reality he is no such thing. That is what I disbelieve. I want to introduce an addition or emendation, and it is one for which Freud has given me the example.

In an earlier lecture (the sixth),[1] after telling us that a psycho-analytic explanation can usually be found for the tunes that we whistle when we seem to be thinking about nothing in particular, Freud adds the following: "I must, however, make this reservation, that I do not maintain this in the case of really musical

[1] Freud, *op. cit.*, p. 80.

people, of whom I happen to have had no experience." This is both honest and penetrating, and leads me to hope that the professor would not have resisted the suggestion that a similar limiting clause would improve his theory of imagination. At any rate that is what I feel that the theory needs. It is true enough, if we do not apply it to imaginative people.

I am ready to admit that there may be human beings whose day-dreams always run in the channels which Freud describes: but surely, for most of us, there has been a fairly clear distinction between two kinds of day-dreams ever since we can remember. With the sort which he acknowledges—the dreams of success, fame, love, and the like—I confess that I am lamentably familiar. I have had dozens of them. But I cannot recall a period when I did not know another kind. The earliest of these which now comes back to me is what might be called the Snug Town. I can see that little town still, with its river and bridge and shipping, the cheeses and barrels piled on the quays, the high-pitched roofs and the bright green shutters. I am vaguer about the inhabitants, but I think they were anthropomorphised Mice—"dressed mice" as I would have called them then, with woollen comforters and wide trousers like Dutchmen, and pipes in their mouths. Obviously most of the images came out of books and the whole thing is quite commonplace. But the point is that I myself was not a feature in it. I dare say that after the dream had taken full possession of me I may have wished, and wished intensely, that I might find this town in reality and go to it. But that was because I had first imagined the town and judged it to be simply delightful, almost adorable, in its own right. My only reason for wishing to go to it was its adorableness: there was no idea that I was to become a great man there, or marry a mouse-princess, or make my fortune out of the local trade in cheeses. And all this time, of course, I was having concurrently the sort of dreams that Freud allows—dreams in which I said clever things, scored off my governess, fought battles, and generally forced the world to acknowledge what a remarkable person I was.

You will have divined that this part of my paper is great fun to write. Who could not go on for hours in the same vein? I wish I had time to tell you of all the other constructions—the unknown room in the house which one was always hoping to discover, the chessmen coming alive as in *Alice*, the garden which was partly in the West and partly in the past—but I reflect that these will hardly interest you as much as they interest me. You would rather write your own ones.

I assume, in fact, that most of you have experienced the same sort of thing, and if you have you will understand me when I say that the two kinds of imagining are really distinguished by their mere taste. We can, if we are challenged, show differences in the content by pointing out that the self is absent from the one and present as hero in the other: but for our own guidance we hardly need to do so. Surely the peculiar "tang" of the merely personal wish-fulfilment is immediately recognisable—its extreme surface realism, its deliberately prosaic temper, and above all its *nagging* character, the stealthy insistence with which it recurs again and again like an anxiety? Surely this is utterly different from the unpredictable ecstasy, the apparent "otherness" and externality of disinterested imagination?

It is worth while, I think, to emphasise the "realism" of the mere wish-fulfilment dream, and to draw the literary consequence that a liberal use of the marvellous, the mythical, and the fantastical in a story is, as far as it goes, an argument *against* the charge of wish-fulfilment. The Freudian fantasy exists to give us the nearest substitute it can for real gratification; naturally it makes itself as lifelike as possible. It had to be unreal as regards the main issue—for we are not really famous men, millionaires or Don Juans—and to make up for this it will be scrupulously "real" everywhere else. Does not all experience confirm this? A man who is really hungry does not dream of honey-dew and elfin bread, but of steak and kidney puddings: a man really lustful does not dream of Titania or Helen, but of real, prosaic, flesh and blood. Other things being equal, a story in which the hero meets Titania and is entertained with fairies' food is much less likely to be a fantasy than "a nice love-story" of which the scene is London, the dialogue idiomatic, and the episodes probable. But this is by the way.

I do not wish to deny that both sorts of day-dream may become the source of literature. I think it probable, for example, that the novels of Charlotte Brontë began as wish-fulfilment dreams, while certain possibly disinterested imaginations about King Julius and the rest, which she shared with her sisters, attempted to express themselves in verse and failed to overcome technical incompetence. Trollope has told us in his *Autobiography*[1] that his novels grew out of what he calls "castle-building" and makes the character of his early reveries quite clear by adding "I myself was of course my own hero". The wish-fulfilling function explains why, as he tells us, "nothing impossible was ever introduced—I never became a king or a duke—I never was a learned man, nor even a philosopher. But I was a very clever person, and beautiful young women used to be fond of me—and altogether I was a very much better fellow than I have ever succeeded in being since." It is, plainly, a text-book case of the self-regarding day-dream. But Trollope significantly adds: "In after years—I have *discarded the hero* of my early dreams and have been able to lay my own identity aside."

This "discarding of the hero" is Trollope's account of what Freud calls the "elaboration" that removes the "grating personal note", and I do not suppose that I am in disagreement with psycho-analysis if I say that, even where a work of art originated in a self-regarding reverie, it becomes art by ceasing to be what

[1] Chapter III.

it was. It is hard to imagine a more radical change than the disappearance of the self who was, by hypothesis, the *raison d'être* of the original dream. The very root from which the dream grew is severed and the dream is planted in a new soil; it is killed as fantasy before it is raised as art. Two other things are worth noting. Trollope's work, which admittedly springs from wish-fulfilment, is work of an unusually solid, realistic, and humdrum kind, which is, on my view, just what we should expect. In the second place, the work is now valued by most readers for just those characters whose fortunes and temperament no one would wish to share, like Bishop Proudie and his wife, or Mr. Crawley and the Archdeacon: whereas the fortunes of the young hero and heroine, where, if anywhere, the last traces of the original self-flattering motive might be expected to survive, are read with indifference.

On these grounds I wish to emend the Freudian theory of literature into something like this. There are two activities of the imagination, one free, and the other enslaved to the wishes of its owner for whom it has to provide imaginary gratifications. Both may be the starting-point for works of art. The former or "free" activity continues in the works it produces and passes from the status of dream to that of art by a process which may legitimately be called "elaboration": incoherences are tidied up, banalities removed, private values and associations replaced, proportion, relief, and temperance are introduced. But the other, or servile kind is not "elaborated" into a work of art: it is a motive power which starts the activity and is withdrawn when once the engine is running, or a scaffolding which is knocked away when the building is complete. Finally, the characteristic products of free imagination belong to what may be roughly called the fantastic, or mythical, or improbable type of literature: those of fantasy, of the wish-fulfilling imagination, to what may, in a very loose sense be called the realistic type. I say "*characteristic* products" because the principle doubtless admits of innumerable exceptions.

By this time I imagine that some of you can hardly contain your laughter at what seems to you the spectacle of a man jumping unconsciously out of the frying-pan into the fire. You have been longing for some time to ask me whether I really suppose that in turning from dreams of power and fame and adult love to dreams of secret rooms, and gardens in the past I have much mended matters; whether I can really be ignorant that all I have done is to exchange dreams that fulfil the comparatively rational and respectable wishes of the Ego for those that fulfil the much darker wishes of the Id. For of course the psycho-analyst will know what to make of that secret room. The garden in the West is child's play to him; and though I do not know how he will explain my town of the Mice, I have no doubt he will make of it something that pertains to infantile sexuality. This brings me to the second of the two Freudian doctrines which I have proposed to discuss: the doctrine of Symbolism.

The doctrine, as stated in the tenth lecture,[1] is this. When we are analysing a dream, that is, when we are trying to find the latent or unconscious thought of which the dream images are a concealed expression, we find some elements with which nothing in the mind of the dreamer is associated. But it fortunately happens that we can find out what such elements are concealing "by drawing", as Freud says, "on our own resources". "Our own resources" apparently means the psycho-analytic examination of folk-lore and language. The result of "drawing on them" is the theory that there are certain things in the real world whose images, when they appear in dreams or stories, bear a constant meaning. That is, whether you or I dream of a house, or read of one in a tale, the latent thought behind the house image is always the same. These images with constant meanings he calls symbols—the words, so to speak, of a universal image-language. He gives us a few specimens. A *House* signifies the human body; *Kings and Queens*,

[1] Freud, *op. cit.*, pp. 125 *et seq.*

fathers and mothers; *Journeys*, death; *small animals* (here come my poor mice, after all, you see) one's brothers and sisters; *Fruit, Landscapes, Gardens, Blossoms*, the female body or various parts of it.

As I have said, I have no intention of disputing with Freud as regards the matter of fact. This is his special subject and as a layman I have no means of finding out whether he is right or wrong; for the purposes of the present argument I am going to assume that he is right as regards fact. But we must be quite clear what it is that I am granting. I am granting three things: (1) That infantile sexual experience of the sort described by Freud does occur in all human beings; (2) That latent thought on such subjects does utilise the images I have mentioned; and (3) which is going very far indeed—that wherever such images occur in dream, imagination, or literature, the latent thought which Freud mentions is really unconsciously present in the mind of the dreamer, the imaginer, and the writer or reader.

I grant all this because if all this were true it would have no literary bearing. All sorts of unconscious thought may be present while we are reading a book—for example, thoughts aroused by the shape of the letters or by the tactual sensations which the paper affords to our fingers—without making our enjoyment other than it seems to be. If latent thought of an erotic character is present in the same irrelevant way whenever I read about a garden, I have, as a critic, no objection. But we reach something much more formidable when Freud says:[1] "Does it not begin to dawn upon us that the many fairy tales which begin with the words 'once upon a time there were a king and queen' simply mean 'once upon a time there were a father and mother'?" *Simply mean* is the crucial expression. They do not "mean" this *inter alia*: they "simply" mean this, this all that they mean, they mean neither more, nor less, nor other, than this.

But how is the word *mean* to be interpreted? We are certainly

[1] *Op. cit.*, p. 134.

not being asked to believe that the teller of the fairy-tale *intends* "king" to be understood as "father", or that the hearer consciously so understands it. I suggest—and let me apologise in advance to all psycho-analysts if I am wrong—that Freud is implicitly making at least the following claims: (1) That the whole of the excitement, pleasure, or interest occasioned by the image, wherever it occurs, is due to the latent erotic thought. (2) That the image, as opposed to the latent thought, effects nothing at all except disguise: or, in other words, that if our inhibitions allowed it to become conscious without shock, the latent thought would give us the same kind and degree of satisfaction as the image now does. It will be seen, of course, that the two claims are really identical: for if the image is anything more than a disguise, if it adds any attractiveness to the latent thought on its own account, then it must follow that the latent thought is not the whole source of the reader's pleasure.

If this is not what Freud means, I have nothing to say to him. But I am sure that this is what is meant by many of his self-styled followers; and it is certainly this, and this alone, which brings psycho-analytic symbolism into contact with literary values. It is in this that the sting lies. We do not mind being told that when we enjoy Milton's description of Eden some latent sexual interest is, as a matter of fact, and along with a thousand other things, present in our unconscious. Our quarrel is with the man who says "you know why you're *really* enjoying this?" or "of course you realise what's behind this?" or "It *all* comes from so-and-so". What we resent, in fact, is not so much the suggestion that we are interested in the female body as the suggestion that we have no interest in gardens: not what the wiseacre would force upon us, but what he threatens to take away. If it is true that all our enjoyment of the images, without remainder, can be explained in terms of infantile sexuality, then, I confess, our literary judgements are in ruins. But I do not believe it is true.

My first argument against it is based on the reaction I have just described—the way in which we find our enjoyments disturbed by the psycho-analyst's suggestion. He may reply that such a reaction of resistance is just what he expected to find and confirms his suspicions. But is this really so ? If the image of a garden is only a disguise for the female body, and if all the excitement with which I read *Paradise Lost*, Book IV, is really erotic, then surely, when the psycho-analyst has kindly removed the veil and conducted me to the thought which (on his view) I was wanting to think all along, I ought to feel not an anticlimax but a climax —the affective temperature ought to rise, not fall ? A man may go to a dinner under the illusion that he wants conversation when he really wants alcohol; but this does not mean that he suddenly loses interest in the proceedings when the champagne appears. He is more likely to realise, as he raises his glass, that this *is* what he really wanted—or at least to find the conversation very much better. It is one thing to admit unconscious desires; it is another to admit desires so unconscious that their satisfaction is felt as a disappointment and an irrelevance. What is the sense in attributing even unconscious thirst to a man who feels less at ease after you have given him drink ? The psycho-analyst will probably reply that our conscious taste rejects his interpretation because of our inhibitions. He would say that the true parallel is not an ordinary man who wants alcohol without knowing it but a fanatical teetotaller who wants alcohol without knowing it; and that such a man might with apparent physical horror reject the champagne when it arrived. In other words, it would be maintained that though, at some level, we "really" wanted to think of the female body, yet our conscious self is so shocked at the disclosure of our real interest that enjoyment ceases.

I am sometimes tempted to wonder whether Freudianism is not a great school of prudery and hypocrisy. The suggestion that we are "shocked" by such interpretations, or that a disgusted recoil is the cause of our resistance, sounds to me like nonsense. I can speak, of course, only for my own sex, and class, and I readily admit that the Viennese ladies who came to consult Freud may have had either chaster or sillier minds than our own: but I can confidently assert that neither I nor anyone I have ever met suffers from such shrinking nausea in the presence of sexual phenomena as the theory seems to demand. I am not speaking of ethics. A man may, of course, have good reason for checking his own thoughts in certain directions or disapproving many of his own actions, but this is something very different from horror. Indeed such a man is likely to look forward with trembling hope to the day when he will become capable of being really shocked, when a light at present inaccessible reveals as essential darkness what still seems to the natural man in him merely ordinary and familiar. To be sure, infantile perversions are in a different category from normal and adult instincts: but I am not sure that even infantile perversions are quite so shocking to us as is claimed. Is not the attitude towards them which Freud assumes something of a public gesture? Does not Freud underrate the extent to which nothing, in private, is really shocking so long as it belongs to ourselves? *Suum cuique bene olet.* . . . I have watched with equanimity the decline and fall of one of my own fingernails at which I would have shuddered in someone else. Again, the feeling with which we reject the psycho-analytic theory of poetry is not one of shock. It is not even a vague disquietude or an unspecified reluctance. It is a quite definite feeling of anticlimax, of frustration. It is not as if we had drawn an embroidered curtain and found earwigs behind it: it is as if we had drawn it expecting to find a whole new wing of the house and found merely a door that led back into the old familiar dining-room. Our feelings would be most unsuitably expressed by the exclamation "Not that!" They demand rather the disappointed grunt "Oh! so that's all".

In general, of course, the fact that a supposed discovery is disappointing does not tend to prove that it is false: but in this question I think it does, for desires and fulfilments and disappointments are what we are discussing. If we are disappointed at finding only sex where we looked for something more, then surely the something more had a value for us? If we are conscious of loss in exchanging the garden for the female body, then clearly the garden added something more than concealment, something positive, to our pleasure. Let us grant that the body was, in fact, concealed behind the garden: yet since the removal of the garden lowers the value of the experience, it follows that the body gained some of its potency by association with the garden. We have not merely removed a veil, we have removed ornaments. Confronted with what is supposed to be the original (the female body) we still prefer the translation—from which any critic must conclude that the translation had merits of its own. Or perhaps "prefer" is the wrong word. We really want both. Poetry is not a substitute for sexual satisfaction, nor sexual satisfaction for poetry. But if so, poetical pleasure is not sexual pleasure *simply* in disguise. It is, at worst, sexual pleasure *plus* something else, and we really want the something else for its own sake.

I now wish to direct your attention to a part of the evidence which is sometimes overlooked. The *Romance of the Rose* seems at first an ideal illustration of the Freudian symbolism, for in it we have not only the garden but the rosebud, which "means" in the second half of the poem exactly what Freud would have it mean. But the trouble is that the whole process here seems to be the wrong way round. The author, and his readers, start with a fully conscious attention to the erotic material and then deliberately express it in the symbols. The symbols do not conceal and are not intended to conceal: they exhibit. The *Romance* may furnish evidence that gardens and rosebuds are excellent symbols for the things Freud has mentioned: but why are any symbols adopted?

It becomes clear that humanity has some motive other than concealment for comparing erotic experience to gardens and flowers: that the erotic experience, thus compared, becomes somehow more interesting—that it is borrowing attractiveness from the flowers, not they from it. And this situation is very common. Donne, in elegies which express quite frankly the most ravenous and unidealised appetite, yet finds that he can improve his poem by comparing his mistress to the earth or to a landscape. Burns tells us that his love is like a red, red rose. These phenomena which might, in a confused glance, be taken to support the Freudian view, are really its refutation. If in the *Romance of the Rose* the erotic thought owes much of its poetical charm to the garden, why should the garden in *Paradise Lost* owe all its poetical charm to the erotic thought? Eroticism on the conscious level seeks not to conceal, but to decorate itself with images taken from gardens. But that which decorates must be, in itself, and for its own sake, pleasing. A necklace of pearls is put around a woman's neck because we think pearls beautiful. If we thought nothing but women beautiful we could not beautify women—we should have no materials with which to do so.

As far as this I think the Freudians are forced to go, and this is enough to save literature. In order to explain the symbols which they themselves insist on we must admit that humanity is interested in many other things besides sex, and that admission is the thin end of the wedge. Once it is allowed that our enjoyment of *Paradise Lost*, Book IV, is a compound of latent erotic interest and real though conscious interest in gardens, then it becomes impossible to say *a priori* in what proportion the two are mixed. And even if it could be shown that the latent erotic interest was as 90 and the interest in gardens as 10, that 10 would still be the subject of literary criticism. For clearly the 10 is what distinguishes one poem from another—the 90 being a monotonous continuum spread under all our reading alike and affording no ground for the distinctions we actually draw between banality and freshness, dullness and charm, ugliness and beauty. For we must remember that a story about a golden dragon plucking the apple of immortality in a garden at the world's end, and a dream about one's pen going through the paper while one scribbles a note, are, in Freudian terms, the same story. But they are not the same as literature.

That is my defence against the psycho-analytic theory of literature taken in its most uncompromising form. A much more civil and humane interpretation of myth and imagery is, however, advanced by Jung, and one which in the pages of Miss Bodkin and Dr. Tillyard has found some interesting critical expression. Indeed I have slipped into it at times myself. It may be called the doctrine of Primordial Images or Archetypal Patterns.

According to Jung[1] there exists, in addition to the individual unconscious, a collective unconscious which is common to the whole human race and even, in some degree, to the whole animal world. Being thus common, it contains the reactions of mind or psyche as such to the most universal situations. Being very primitive, it is pre-logical and its reactions are expressed not in thought but in images. Myths, or at any rate the older and greater myths, are such images recovered from the collective unconscious. Their power of moving us—which Jung himself obviously experiences in a very high degree—is explained as follows:

If this supra-individual mind exists, everything that is translated into its picture speech would be depersonalised and, if it became conscious, would appear to us *sub specie aeternitatis*. Not as my sorrow, but as the sorrow of the world, not a personal isolating pain, but a pain without bitterness that unites all humanity. That this can help us needs no proof.[2]

[1] *Contributions to Analytical Psychology*, trans. H. G. and C. F. Baynes (Kegan Paul, London, 1928), "Mind and the Earth," pp. 27 *et seq.*

[2] Jung, *op. cit.*, p. 108.

You will gather that Jung, when he wrote that sentence, was thinking mainly of collective reactions to painful situations, expressed in tragic myths: to complete his argument we should therefore add a similar explanation about the joyous myths "Not as my joy, but as the joy of the world, &c.".

The most interesting thing about this theory is the strength of the emotional reaction it awakes in nearly all those who hear it. Before its scientific merits have been considered, some are instantly repelled; they have a sense of being lured by sirens or got at by mystagogues; they feel something between fright and contempt; and they resolve to remain, at all costs, outside the magic circle, to stick to modern, self-conscious, self-explanatory aesthetics. Others, with equal suddenness, are enchanted: every half-conscious expectation which they have formed in the presence of great art seems to be fulfilled, and their hearts are enlisted on the side of the theory before their heads have had time to examine it. Let me confess at once that I belong, by temperament, to the second group, but have, by my training, acquired a certain sympathy with the first. Thanks to my training I can suspend my judgement about the scientific value of Jung's essay on "Mind and the Earth": but I perceive at once that even if it turns out to be bad science it is excellent poetry.

This brings us to a most important point—to nothing less, if I were qualified to carry it out, than the psycho-analysis of psycho-analysis itself. Such a hyper-analysis ought to be limited as Freud limited his analysis of whistling, no doubt; it would not refer to "really scientific people", but to the great mass of ordinary people who read psycho-analytic books with avidity and undergo their influence. I do not think we can doubt that for such people psycho-analysis itself satisfies certain very strong emotional needs. I have just stated Jung's theory in the coldest and least evocative language I could find: let us now see it as it actually appears in the essay on "Mind and the Earth".

We have to deal with the beginnings and *foundations* of the mind, with *things that from immemorial time have lain buried in the depths* . . . the unexpected question *whether the unconscious also has dreams* . . . are there resultants of *yet deeper and, if possible, more unconscious* processes? . . . altogether *too adventurous* . . . this mind of *venerable age* . . . a rationalist may laugh, but *something deep* is stirred in us . . . those *far-away* backgrounds, those *most ancient* forms . . . inherited from the *dim ages* of the past . . . I have found that an intellectual apprehension of these things in no way detracts from their value; on the contrary, it helps us not only to feel, but to comprehend their *immense significance* . . . *not idly* did Faust say "*The Mothers! The Mothers! it sounds so strange*".

Do not for one moment suppose that I am laughing at Jung: but, quite frankly, my unreflective reaction to all this can only be expressed in some such words as "Isn't this grand?" *Agnosco veteris vestigia flammae!* Something dim and far removed—buried in the depths from immemorial time—stirring beneath the surface—coming to life—coming up at last—well, I know where I am now. I am with Schliemann digging up what he believed to be the very bones of Agamemnon, king of men: I am with Collingwood discovering behind the Arthurian stories some far-off echo of real happenings in the thick darkness of British history: with Asia in the fourth act of *Prometheus* following her dream down, down into the cave of Demogorgon: with Wordsworth, sinking deep and ascending into regions "to which the heaven of heavens is but a veil": with Alice, finding beneath the curtain the little door which she could not pass, which led to the delectable garden: with my own past self, hoping, as a child, for that forgotten, that undiscovered, room. I am with British Israelites and Baconians and historians of Atlantis, with Renaissance magicians and seekers for the sources of the Nile. In a word I am enjoying myself immensely; but the point I wish to make is simply this: that Jung's discussion of "primordial images" itself awakes a primordial image of the first water: that Miss Bodkin's

Archetypal Patterns[1] itself exhibits an archetypal pattern of extreme potency.

I trust that you recognise which it is; it might be called the Recovery Pattern, or the Veiled Isis, or the Locked Door, or the Lost-and-Found. The Freudians will explain it in terms of infantile sexual curiosity—indeed I have seen Alice and the curtained door so explained—but that need not bother us. Such curiosity may, in the life of each one of us, have been the earliest embodiment of it, for all I know: but since then we have learned to prefer it in several more exciting and less obvious forms—the thirst which it kindles in us has long outrun "those perishing waters". It is, indeed, an image inevitably embodying certain absolutely universal features of our experience, religious, intellectual, aesthetic, and sexual alike.

The presence of such a primordial image in the psycho-analytic process itself is, I think, the explanation of its popularity—for the same image is aroused by Freudian analysis too. In this respect psycho-analysis heals some of the wounds made by materialism. For the general effect of materialism is to give you, where you expected an indefinite depth of reality, a flat wall only a few inches away. Psycho-analysis offers you some kind of depth back again—lots of things hidden behind the wall. Hence those who have once tasted it feel that they are being robbed of something if we try to take it from them.

The emotional power of Jung's essay is, as far as it goes, a proof that he is quite right in claiming that certain images, in whatever material they are embodied, have a strange power to excite the human mind. Every sentence he writes helps to prove this. At the same time we may be cautious about accepting his explanation, since there are some grounds of suspecting that the argument seems plausible not because of its real cogency but because of the

[1] *Archetypal Patterns in Poetry*. Maud Bodkin (London, Oxford University Press, 1934).

powerful emotions it arouses. Has Jung, in fact, worked us into a
state of mind in which almost anything, provided it was dim,
remote, long buried, and mysterious, would seem (for the moment) an adequate explanation of the "leap in our blood" which
responds to great myth?

Let us look at the matter in cold prose. We want to know why
certain images are exciting. Jung replies, "because they are
ancient, because, in contemplating them, we are doing what our
prehistoric ancestors did". Now the *idea* that we are doing so is
certainly exciting, as all ideas of antiquity are. But this idea is not
necessarily entertained by the man in the moment of responding
to a myth. He may not have read Jung's theory; he may think
that what he is contemplating is quite new: he may not raise the
question of its age at all. Nevertheless he will respond. If Jung is
right, then, it is not the *idea* of following our remote ancestors
which produces the response but the mere *fact* of doing so,
whether we are conscious of this fact or no. But there is no evidence that the actual reproduction of prehistoric behaviour, apart
from the reflection that we are reproducing it, is at all exciting
or impressive. We reproduce very ancient modes of behaviour in
all our humblest animal operations. We are at one with our pre-
Adamite sires when we scratch; and though I have no wish to
underrate the pleasures of a good scratch, I think them very unlike those of a good poem. No doubt even scratching may be
made poetical if we reflect on the antiquity of the practice: but
the pleasure we shall then get will not be the pleasure of scratching
(the οἰκεία ἡδονή) but the pleasure of historico-poetical medita-
tion. In the same way, I suggest, Jung has not explained the
pleasure of entertaining primordial images but exhibited the
pleasure of meditating on them and of entertaining, in the process,
one particular primordial image, which itself needs explanation
as much as any of the others. The *idea* that our sorrow is part of
the world's sorrow is, in certain moods, moving enough: the

mere *fact* that lots of other people have had toothache does not make toothache less painful.

I have no answer to the question Jung has raised. I can only say—indulging once more in the same primordial image—that the mystery of primordial images is deeper, their origin more remote, their cave more hid, their fountain less accessible than those suspect who have yet dug deepest, sounded with the longest cord, or journeyed farthest in the wilderness—for why should I not be allowed to write in this vein as well as everyone else?

A Paper at Westfield College, 1941

8

The Inner Ring

MAY I read you a few lines from Tolstoi's *War and Peace*?

When Boris entered the room, Prince Andrey was listening to an old general, wearing his decorations, who was reporting something to Prince Andrey, with an expression of soldierly servility on his purple face. "Alright. Please wait!" he said to the general, speaking in Russian with the French accent which he used when he spoke with contempt. The moment he noticed Boris he stopped listening to the general who trotted imploringly after him and begged to be heard, while Prince Andrey turned to Boris with a cheerful smile and a nod of the head. Boris now clearly understood—what he had already guessed—that side by side with the system of discipline and subordination which were laid down in the Army Regulations, there existed a different and a more real system—the system which compelled a tightly laced general with a purple face to wait respectfully for his turn while a mere captain like Prince Andrey chatted with a mere second lieutenant like Boris. Boris decided at once that he would be guided not by the official system but by this other unwritten system.[1]

When you invite a middle-aged moralist to address you, I suppose I must conclude, however unlikely the conclusion seems, that you have a taste for middle-aged moralising. I shall do my best to gratify it. I shall in fact give you advice about the world in which you are going to live. I do not mean by this that I am going to attempt a talk on what are called current affairs. You probably know quite as much about them as I do. I am not going to tell you—except in a form so general that you will hardly recognise

[1] Part III, Chapter 9.

it—what part you ought to play in post-war reconstruction. It is not, in fact, very likely that any of you will be able, in the next ten years, to make any direct contribution to the peace or prosperity of Europe. You will be busy finding jobs, getting married, acquiring facts. I am going to do something more old-fashioned than you perhaps expected. I am going to give advice. I am going to issue warnings. Advice and warnings about things which are so perennial that no one calls them "current affairs".

And of course everyone knows what a middle-aged moralist of my type warns his juniors against. He warns them against the World, the Flesh, and the Devil. But one of this trio will be enough to deal with today. The Devil, I shall leave strictly alone. The association between him and me in the public mind has already gone quite as deep as I wish: in some quarters it has already reached the level of confusion, if not of identification. I begin to realise the truth of the old proverb that he who sups with that formidable host needs a long spoon. As for the Flesh, you must be very abnormal young people if you do not know quite as much about it as I do. But on the World I think I have something to say.

In the passage I have just read from Tolstoi, the young second lieutenant Boris Dubretskoi discovers that there exist in the army two different systems or hierarchies. The one is printed in some little red book and anyone can easily read it up. It also remains constant. A general is always superior to a colonel and a colonel to a captain. The other is not printed anywhere. Nor is it even a formally organised secret society with officers and rules which you would be told after you had been admitted. You are never formally and explicitly admitted by anyone. You discover gradually, in almost indefinable ways, that it exists and that you are outside it; and then later, perhaps, that you are inside it. There are what correspond to passwords, but they too are spontaneous and informal. A particular slang, the use of particular nicknames, an allusive manner of conversation, are the marks. But it is not constant. It is not easy, even at a given moment, to say who is inside and who is outside. Some people are obviously in and some are obviously out, but there are always several on the border-line. And if you come back to the same Divisional Headquarters, or Brigade Headquarters, or the same regiment or even the same company, after six weeks' absence, you may find this second hierarchy quite altered. There are no formal admissions or expulsions. People think they are in it after they have in fact been pushed out of it, or before they have been allowed in: this provides great amusement for those who are really inside. It has no fixed name. The only certain rule is that the insiders and outsiders call it by different names. From inside it may be designated, in simple cases, by mere enumeration: it may be called "You and Tony and me". When it is very secure and comparatively stable in membership it calls itself "we". When it has to be suddenly expanded to meet a particular emergency it calls itself "All the sensible people at this place". From outside, if you have despaired of getting into it, you call it "That gang" or "They" or "So-and-so and his set" or "the Caucus" or "the Inner Ring". If you are a candidate for admission you probably don't call it anything. To discuss it with the other outsiders would make you feel outside yourself. And to mention it in talking to the man who is inside, and who may help you in if this present conversation goes well, would be madness.

Badly as I may have described it, I hope you will all have recognised the thing I am describing. Not, of course, that you have been in the Russian Army or perhaps in any army. But you have met the phenomenon of an Inner Ring. You discovered one in your house at school before the end of the first term. And when you had climbed up to somewhere near it by the end of your second year, perhaps you discovered that within the Ring there was a Ring yet more inner, which in its turn was the fringe of the great school Ring to which the house Rings were only satellites. It is even possible that the School Ring was almost in touch with a Masters' Ring. You were beginning, in fact, to pierce through the skins of the onion. And here, too, at your university —shall I be wrong in assuming that at this very moment, invisible to me, there are several rings—independent systems or concentric rings—present in this room? And I can assure you that in whatever hospital, inn of court, diocese, school, business, or college you arrive after going down, you will find the Rings—what Tolstoi calls the second or unwritten systems.

All this is rather obvious. I wonder whether you will say the same of my next step, which is this. I believe that in all men's lives at certain periods, and in many men's lives at all periods between infancy and extreme old age, one of the most dominant elements is the desire to be inside the local Ring and the terror of being left outside. This desire, in one of its forms, has indeed had ample justice done to it in literature. I mean, in the form of snobbery. Victorian fiction is full of characters who are hag-ridden by the desire to get inside that particular Ring which is, or was, called Society. But it must be clearly understood that "Society", in that sense of the word, is merely one of a hundred Rings and snobbery therefore only one form of the longing to be inside. People who believe themselves to be free, and indeed are free, from snobbery, and who read satires on snobbery with tranquil superiority, may be devoured by the desire in another form. It may be the very intensity of their desire to enter some quite different Ring which renders them immune from the allurements of high life. An invitation from a duchess would be very cold comfort to a man smarting under the sense of exclusion from some artistic or communist côterie. Poor man—it is not large, lighted rooms, or champagne, or even scandals about peers and Cabinet Ministers that he wants: it is the sacred little attic or studio, the heads bent together, the fog of tobacco smoke, and the delicious knowledge that we—we four or five all huddled beside this stove—are the people who *know*. Often the desire conceals itself so well that we hardly recognise the pleasures of fruition. Men tell not only their wives but themselves that it is a hardship to stay late at the office or the school on some bit of important extra work which they have been let in for because they and So-and-so and the two others are the only people left in the place who really know how things are run. But it is not quite true. It is a terrible bore, of course, when old Fatty Smithson draws you aside and whispers "Look here, we've got to get you in on this examination somehow" or "Charles and I saw at once that you've got to be on this committee". A terrible bore ... ah, but how much more terrible if you were left out! It is tiring and unhealthy to lose your Saturday afternoons: but to have them free because you don't matter, that is much worse.

Freud would say, no doubt, that the whole thing is a subterfuge of the sexual impulse. I wonder whether the shoe is not sometimes on the other foot, I wonder whether, in ages of promiscuity, many a virginity has not been lost less in obedience to Venus than in obedience to the lure of the caucus. For of course, when promiscuity is the fashion, the chaste are outsiders. They are ignorant of something that other people know. They are uninitiated. And as for lighter matters, the number who first smoked or first got drunk for a similar reason is probably very large.

I must now make a distinction. I am not going to say that the existence of Inner Rings is an evil. It is certainly unavoidable. There must be confidential discussions: and it is not only not a bad thing, it is (in itself) a good thing, that personal friendship should grow up between those who work together. And it is perhaps impossible that the official hierarchy of any organisation should quite coincide with its actual workings. If the wisest and most energetic people invariably held the highest posts, it might coincide; since they often do not, there must be people in high

143

positions who are really deadweights and people in lower positions who are more important than their rank and seniority would
lead you to suppose. In that way the second, unwritten system is
bound to grow up. It is necessary; and perhaps it is not a necessary
evil. But the desire which draws us into Inner Rings is another
matter. A thing may be morally neutral and yet the desire for
that thing may be dangerous. As Byron has said:

> Sweet is a legacy, and passing sweet
> The unexpected death of some old lady.

The painless death of a pious relative at an advanced age is not
an evil. But an earnest desire for her death on the part of her heirs
is not reckoned a proper feeling, and the law frowns on even the
gentlest attempt to expedite her departure. Let Inner Rings be an
unavoidable and even an innocent feature of life, though certainly
not a beautiful one: but what of our longing to enter them, our
anguish when we are excluded, and the kind of pleasure we feel
when we get in?

I have no right to make assumptions about the degree to which
any of you may already be compromised. I must not assume that
you have ever first neglected, and finally shaken off, friends whom
you really loved and who might have lasted you a lifetime,
in order to court the friendship of those who appeared to you
more important, more esoteric. I must not ask whether you have
ever derived actual pleasure from the loneliness and humiliation
of the outsiders after you yourself were in: whether you have
talked to fellow members of the Ring in the presence of outsiders
simply in order that the outsiders might envy; whether the means
whereby, in your days of probation, you propitiated the Inner
Ring, were always wholly admirable. I will ask only one question
—and it is, of course, a rhetorical question which expects no
answer. In the whole of your life as you now remember it,
has the desire to be on the right side of that invisible line ever

prompted you to any act or word on which, in the cold small hours of a wakeful night, you can look back with satisfaction? If so, your case is more fortunate than most.

But I said I was going to give advice, and advice should deal with the future, not the past. I have hinted at the past only to awake you to what I believe to be the real nature of human life. I don't believe that the economic motive and the erotic motive account for everything that goes on in what we moralists call the World. Even if you add Ambition I think the picture is still incomplete. The lust for the esoteric, the longing to be inside, take many forms which are not easily recognisable as Ambition. We hope, no doubt, for tangible profits from every Inner Ring we penetrate: power, money, liberty to break rules, avoidance of routine duties, evasion of discipline. But all these would not satisfy us if we did not get in addition the delicious sense of secret intimacy. It is no doubt a great convenience to know that we need fear no official reprimands from our official senior because he is old Percy, a fellow-member of our Ring. But we don't value the intimacy only for the sake of convenience; quite equally we value the convenience as a proof of the intimacy.

My main purpose in this address is simply to convince you that this desire is one of the great permanent mainsprings of human action. It is one of the factors which go to make up the world as we know it—this whole pell-mell of struggle, competition, con-fusion, graft, disappointment and advertisement, and if it is one of the permanent mainsprings then you may be quite sure of this. Unless you take measures to prevent it, this desire is going to be one of the chief motives of your life, from the first day on which you enter your profession until the day when you are too old to care. That will be the natural thing—the life that will come to you of its own accord. Any other kind of life, if you lead it, will be the result of conscious and continuous effort. If you do nothing about it, if you drift with the stream, you will in fact be an "inner ringer". I don't say you'll be a successful one; that's as may be. But whether by pining and moping outside Rings that you can never enter, or by passing triumphantly further and further in— one way or the other you will be that kind of man.

I have already made it fairly clear that I think it better for you not to be that kind of man. But you may have an open mind on the question. I will therefore suggest two reasons for thinking as I do.

It would be polite and charitable, and in view of your age reasonable too, to suppose that none of you is yet a scoundrel. On the other hand, by the mere law of averages (I am saying nothing against free will) it is almost certain that at least two or three of you before you die will have become something very like scoundrels. There must be in this room the makings of at least that number of unscrupulous, treacherous, ruthless egotists. The choice is still before you: and I hope you will not take my hard words about your possible future characters as a token of disrespect to your present characters. And the prophecy I make is this. To nine out of ten of you the choice which could lead to scoundrelism will come, when it does come, in no very dramatic colours. Obviously bad men, obviously threatening or bribing, will almost certainly not appear. Over a drink or a cup of coffee, disguised as a triviality and sandwiched between two jokes, from the lips of a man, or woman, whom you have recently been getting to know rather better and whom you hope to know better still—just at the moment when you are most anxious not to appear crude, or naïf or a prig—the hint will come. It will be the hint of something which is not quite in accordance with the technical rules of fair play: something which the public, the ignorant, romantic public, would never understand: something which even the outsiders in your own profession are apt to make a fuss about: but something, says your new friend, which "we" —and at the word "we" you try not to blush for mere pleasure

—something "we always do". And you will be drawn in, if you are drawn in, not by desire for gain or ease, but simply because at that moment, when the cup was so near your lips, you cannot bear to be thrust back again into the cold outer world. It would be so terrible to see the other man's face—that genial, confidential, delightfully sophisticated face—turn suddenly cold and contemptuous, to know that you had been tried for the Inner Ring and rejected. And then, if you are drawn in, next week it will be something a little further from the rules, and next year something further still, but all in the jolliest, friendliest spirit. It may end in a crash, a scandal, and penal servitude: it may end in millions, a peerage and giving the prizes at your old school. But you will be a scoundrel.

That is my first reason. Of all passions the passion for the Inner Ring is most skilful in making a man who is not yet a very bad man do very bad things.

My second reason is this. The torture allotted to the Danaids in the classical underworld, that of attempting to fill sieves with water, is the symbol not of one vice but of all vices. It is the very mark of a perverse desire that it seeks what is not to be had. The desire to be inside the invisible line illustrates this rule. As long as you are governed by that desire you will never get what you want. You are trying to peel an onion: if you succeed there will be nothing left. Until you conquer the fear of being an outsider, an outsider you will remain.

This is surely very clear when you come to think of it. If you want to be made free of a certain circle for some wholesome reason—if, say, you want to join a musical society because you really like music—then there is a possibility of satisfaction. You may find yourself playing in a quartet and you may enjoy it. But if all you want is to be in the know, your pleasure will be short-lived. The circle cannot have from within the charm it had from outside. By the very act of admitting you it has lost its magic. Once the first novelty is worn off the members of this circle will be no more interesting than your old friends. Why should they be? You were not looking for virtue or kindness or loyalty or humour or learning or wit or any of the things that can be really enjoyed. You merely wanted to be "in". And that is a pleasure than cannot last. As soon as your new associates have been staled to you by custom, you will be looking for another Ring. The rainbow's end will still be ahead of you. The old Ring will now be only the drab background for your endeavour to enter the new one.

And you will always find them hard to enter, for a reason you very well know. You yourself, once you are in, want to make it hard for the next entrant, just as those who are already in made it hard for you. Naturally. In any wholesome group of people which holds together for a good purpose, the exclusions are in a sense accidental. Three or four people who are together for the sake of some piece of work exclude others because there is work only for so many or because the others can't in fact do it. Your little musical group limits its numbers because the rooms they meet in are only so big. But your genuine Inner Ring exists for exclusion. There'd be no fun if there were no outsiders. The invisible line would have no meaning unless most people were on the wrong side of it. Exclusion is no accident: it is the essence.

The quest of the Inner Ring will break your hearts unless you break it. But if you break it, a surprising result will follow. If in your working hours you make the work your end, you will presently find yourself all unawares inside the only circle in your profession that really matters. You will be one of the sound craftsmen, and other sound craftsmen will know it. This group of craftsmen will by no means coincide with the Inner Ring or the Important People or the People in the Know. It will not shape that professional policy or work up that professional influence which fights for the profession as a whole against the public:

nor will it lead to those periodic scandals and crises which the Inner Ring produces. But it will do those things which that profession exists to do and will in the long run be responsible for all the respect which that profession in fact enjoys and which the speeches and advertisements cannot maintain. And if in your spare time you consort simply with the people you like, you will again find that you have come unawares to a real inside: that you are indeed snug and safe at the centre of something which, seen from without, would look exactly like an Inner Ring. But the difference is that its secrecy is accidental, and its exclusiveness a by-product, and no one was led thither by the lure of the esoteric: for it is only four or five people who like one another meeting to do things that they like. This is friendship. Aristotle placed it among the virtues. It causes perhaps half of all the happiness in the world, and no Inner Ringer can ever have it.

We are told in Scripture that those who ask get. That is true, in senses I can't now explore. But in another sense there is much truth in the schoolboy's principle "them as asks shan't have". To a young person, just entering on adult life, the world seems full of "insides", full of delightful intimacies and confidentialities, and he desires to enter them. But if he follows that desire he will reach no "inside" that is worth reaching. The true road lies in quite another direction. It is like the house in *Alice Through the Looking Glass.*

Memorial Oration at King's College, London, 1944

9

Is Theology Poetry?

THE QUESTION I have been asked to discuss tonight—"Is Theology Poetry?"—is not of my own choosing. I find myself, in fact, in the position of a candidate at an examination; and I must obey the advice of my tutors by first making sure that I know what the question means.

By Theology we mean, I suppose, the systematic series of statements about God and about man's relation to Him which the believers of a religion make. And in a paper set me by this Club I may perhaps assume that Theology means principally Christian Theology. I am the bolder to make this assumption because something of what I think about other religions will appear in what I have to say. It must also be remembered that only a minority of the religions of the world have a theology. There was no systematic series of statements which the Greeks agreed in believing about Zeus.

The other term, Poetry, is much harder to define, but I believe I can assume the question which my examiners had in mind without a definition. There are certain things which I feel sure they were not asking me. They were not asking me whether Theology is written in verse. They were not asking me whether most theologians are masters of a "simple, sensuous and passionate" style. I believe they meant: "Is Theology *merely* poetry?" This might be expanded: "Does Theology offer us, at best, only that kind of truth which, according to some critics, poetry offers us?" And the first difficulty of answering the question in that form is that we have no general agreement as to what "poetical truth" means, or whether there is really any such thing. It will be best, therefore, to use for this paper a very vague and modest notion of poetry, simply as writing which arouses and in part satisfies the imagination. And I shall take it that the question I am to answer is this: Does Christian Theology owe its attraction to its power of arousing and satisfying our imaginations? Are those who believe it mistaking aesthetic enjoyment for intellectual assent, or assenting because they enjoy?

Faced with this question, I naturally turn to inspect the believer whom I know best—myself. And the first fact I discover, or seem to discover, is that for me at any rate, if Theology is Poetry, it is not very good poetry.

Considered as poetry, the doctrine of the Trinity seems to me to fall between two stools. It has neither the monolithic grandeur of strictly Unitarian conceptions, nor the richness of Polytheism. The omnipotence of God is not, to my taste, a poetical advantage. Odin, fighting against enemies who are not his own creatures and who will in fact defeat him in the end, has a heroic appeal which the God of the Christians cannot have. There is also a certain bareness about the Christian picture of the universe. A future state, and orders of superhuman creatures, are held to exist, but only the slightest hints of their nature are offered. Finally, and worst of all, the whole cosmic story though full of tragic elements yet fails of being a tragedy. Christianity offers the attractions neither of optimism nor of pessimism. It represents the life of the universe as being very like the mortal life of men on this planet —"of a mingled yarn, good and ill together". The majestic simplifications of Pantheism and the tangled wood of Pagan animism both seem to me, in their different ways, more attractive. Christianity just misses the tidiness of the one and the delicious variety of the other. For I take it there are two things the imagination loves to do. It loves to embrace its object completely, to take it in at a single glance and see it as something harmonious, symmetrical and self-explanatory. That is the classical imagination: the Parthenon was built for it. It also loves to lose itself in a labyrinth, to surrender to the inextricable. That is the romantic imagination: the *Orlando Furioso* was written for it. But Christian Theology does not cater very well for either.

If Christianity is only a mythology, then I find the mythology I believe in is not the one I like best. I like Greek mythology much better: Irish better still: Norse best of all.

Having thus inspected myself, I next inquire how far my case is peculiar. It does not seem, certainly, to be unique. It is not at all plain that men's imaginations have always delighted most in those pictures of the supernatural which they believed. From the twelfth to the seventeenth century Europe seems to have taken an unfailing delight in classical mythology. If the numbers and the gusto of pictures and poems were to be the criterion of belief, we should judge that those ages were pagan; which we know to be untrue.

It looks as if the confusion between imaginative enjoyment and intellectual assent, of which Christians are accused, is not nearly so common or so easy as some people suppose. Even children, I believe, rarely suffer from it. It pleases their imagination to pretend that they are bears or horses; but I do not remember that one was ever under the least delusion. May it not even be that there is something in belief which is hostile to perfect imaginative enjoyment? The sensitive, cultured atheist seems at times to enjoy the aesthetic trappings of Christianity in a way which the believer can only envy. The modern poets certainly enjoy the Greek gods in a way of which I find no trace in Greek literature. What mythological scenes in ancient literature can compare for a moment with Keats's *Hyperion*? In a certain sense we spoil a mythology for imaginative purposes by believing in it. Fairies are popular in England because we don't think they exist; they are no fun at all in Arran or Connemara.

But I must beware of going too far. I have suggested that belief spoils a system for the imagination "in a certain sense". But not in all senses. If I came to believe in fairies I should almost certainly lose the particular kind of pleasure which I now get from them when reading the *Midsummer Night's Dream*. But later on, when the believed fairies had settled down as inhabitants of my real universe and had been fully connected with other parts of my thought, a new pleasure might arise. The contemplation of what we take to be real is always, I think, in tolerably sensitive minds, attended with a certain sort of aesthetic satisfaction—a sort which depends precisely on its supposed reality. There is a dignity and poignancy in the bare fact that a thing exists. Thus, as Balfour pointed out in *Theism and Humanism* (a book too little read) there are many historical facts which we should not applaud for any obvious humour or pathos if we supposed them to be inventions; but once we believe them to be real we have, in addition to our intellectual satisfaction, a certain aesthetic delight in the idea of them. The story of the Trojan War and the story of the Napoleonic Wars both have an aesthetic effect on us. And the effects are different. And this difference does not depend solely on those differences which would make them different as stories if we believed neither. The *kind* of pleasure the Napoleonic Wars give has a certain difference simply because we believe in them. A believed idea *feels* different from an idea that is not believed. And that peculiar flavour of the believed is never, in my experience, without a special sort of imaginative enjoyment. It is therefore quite true that the Christians do enjoy their world picture, aesthetically, once they have accepted it as true. Every man, I believe, enjoys the world picture which he accepts: for the gravity and finality of the actual is itself an aesthetic stimulus. In this sense, Christianity, Life-Force-Worship, Marxism, Freudianism all become "poetries" to their own believers. But this does not mean that their adherents have chosen them for that reason. On the contrary, this kind of poetry is the result, not the cause, of belief. Theology is, in this sense, poetry to me because I believe it: I do not believe it because it is poetry.

The charge that Theology is mere poetry, if it means that Christians believe it because they find it, antecedently to belief, the most poetically attractive of all world pictures, thus seems to me unplausible in the extreme. There may be evidence for such a charge which I do not know of: but such evidence as I do know is against it.

I am not of course maintaining that Theology, even before you believe it, is totally bare of aesthetic value. But I do not find it superior in this respect to most of its rivals. Consider for a few moments the enormous aesthetic claim of its chief contemporary rival—what we may loosely call the Scientific Outlook,[1] the picture of Mr. Wells and the rest. Supposing this to be a myth, is it not one of the finest myths which human imagination has yet produced? The play is preceded by the most austere of all preludes: the infinite void, and matter restlessly moving to bring forth it knows not what. Then, by the millionth millionth chance —what tragic irony—the conditions at one point of space and time bubble up into that tiny fermentation which is the beginning of life. Everything seems to be against the infant hero of our drama—just as everything seems against the youngest son or ill-used stepdaughter at the opening of a fairy-tale. But life somehow wins through. With infinite suffering, against all but insuperable obstacles, it spreads, it breeds, it complicates itself: from the amoeba up to the plant, up to the reptile, up to the mammal. We glance briefly at the age of monsters. Dragons prowl the earth, devour one another and die. Then comes the theme of the younger son and the ugly duckling once more. As the weak,

[1] I am not suggesting that practising scientists believe it as a whole. The delightful name 'Wellsianity'. (which another member invented during the discussion) would have been much better than 'the Scientific Outlook'.

tiny spark of life began amidst the huge hostilities of the inanimate, so now again, amidst the beasts that are far larger and stronger than he, there comes forth a little naked, shivering, cowering creature, shuffling, not yet erect, promising nothing: the product of another millionth millionth chance. Yet somehow he thrives. He becomes the Cave Man with his club and his flints, muttering and growling over his enemies' bones, dragging his screaming mate by her hair (I never could quite make out why), tearing his children to pieces in fierce jealousy till one of them is old enough to tear him, cowering before the horrible gods whom he has created in his own image. But these are only growing pains. Wait till the next Act. There he is becoming true Man. He learns to master Nature. Science comes and dissipates the superstitions of his infancy. More and more he becomes the controller of his own fate. Passing hastily over the present (for it is a mere nothing by the time-scale we are using), you follow him on into the future. See him in the last act, though not the last scene, of this great mystery. A race of demigods now rule the planet—and perhaps more than the planet—for eugenics have made certain that only demigods will be born, and psycho-analysis that none of them shall lose or smirch his divinity, and communism that all which divinity requires shall be ready to their hands. Man has ascended his throne. Henceforward he has nothing to do but to practise virtue, to grow in wisdom, to be happy. And now, mark the final stroke of genius. If the myth stopped at that point, it might be a little bathetic. It would lack the highest grandeur of which human imagination is capable. The last scene reverses all. We have the Twilight of the Gods. All this time, silently, unceasingly, out of all reach of human power, Nature, the old enemy, has been steadily gnawing away. The sun will cool—all suns will cool—the whole universe will run down. Life (every form of life) will be banished, without hope of return, from every inch of infinite space. All ends in nothingness, and "universal darkness covers all". The pattern of the myth thus becomes one of the noblest we can conceive. It is the pattern of many Elizabethan tragedies, where the protagonist's career can be represented by a slowly ascending and then rapidly falling curve, with its highest point in Act IV. You see him climbing up and up, then blazing in his bright meridian, then finally overwhelmed in ruin.

Such a world-drama appeals to every part of us. The early struggles of the hero (a theme delightfully doubled, played first by life, and then by man) appeals to our generosity. His future exaltation gives scope to a reasonable optimism; for the tragic close is so very distant that you need not often think of it—we work with millions of years. And the tragic close itself just gives that irony, that grandeur, which calls forth our defiance, and without which all the rest might cloy. There is a beauty in this myth which well deserves better poetic handling than it has yet received: I hope some great genius will yet crystallise it before the incessant stream of philosophic change carries it all away. I am speaking, of course, of the beauty it has whether you believe it or not. There I can speak from experience: for I, who believe less than half of what it tells me about the past, and less than nothing of what it tells me about the future, am deeply moved when I contemplate it. The only other story—unless, indeed, it is an embodiment of the same story—which similarly moves me is the *Nibelung's Ring. Enden sah ich die Welt.*

We cannot, therefore, turn down Theology, simply because it does not avoid being poetical. All world views yield poetry to those who believe them by the mere fact of being believed. And nearly all have certain poetical merits whether you believe them or not. This is what we should expect. Man is a poetical animal and touches nothing which he does not adorn.

There are, however, two other lines of thought which might lead us to call Theology a mere poetry, and these I must now consider. In the first place, it certainly contains elements similar to those which we find in many early, and even savage, religions. And those elements in the early religions may now seem to us to be poetical. The question here is rather complicated. We now regard the death and return of Balder as a poetical idea, a myth. We are invited to infer thence that the death and resurrection of Christ is a poetical idea, a myth. But we are not really starting with the *datum* "Both are poetical" and thence arguing "Therefore both are false". Part of the poetical aroma which hangs about Balder is, I believe, due to the fact that we have already come to disbelieve in him. So that disbelief, not poetical experience, is the real starting point of the argument. But this is perhaps an over-subtlety, certainly a subtlety, and I will leave it on one side.

What light is really thrown on the truth or falsehood of Christtian Theology by the occurrence of similar ideas in Pagan religion? I think the answer was very well given a fortnight ago by Mr. Brown. Supposing, for purposes of argument, that Christtianity is true, then it could avoid all coincidence with other religions only on the supposition that all other religions are one hundred per cent erroneous. To which, you remember, Professor Price replied by agreeing with Mr. Brown and saying: "Yes. From these resemblances you may conclude not 'so much the worse for the Christians' but 'so much the better for the Pagans'." The truth is that the resemblances tell nothing either for or against the truth of Christian Theology. If you start from the assumption that the Theology is false, the resemblances are quite consistent with that assumption. One would expect creatures of the same sort, faced with the same universe, to make the same false guess more than once. But if you start with the assumption that the Theology is true, the resemblances fit in equally well. Theology, while saying that a special illumination has been vouchsafed to Christians and (earlier) to Jews, also says that there is some

157

divine illumination vouchsafed to all men. The Divine light, we are told, "lighteneth every man". We should, therefore, expect to find in the imagination of great Pagan teachers and myth-makers some glimpse of that theme which we believe to be the very plot of the whole cosmic story—the theme of incarnation, death and re-birth. And the differences between the Pagan Christs (Balder, Osiris, etc.) and the Christ Himself is much what we should expect to find. The Pagan stories are all about someone dying and rising, either every year, or else nobody knows where and nobody knows when. The Christian story is about a historical personage, whose execution can be dated pretty accurately, under a named Roman magistrate, and with whom the society that He founded is in a continuous relation down to the present day. It is not the difference between falsehood and truth. It is the difference between a real event on the one hand and dim dreams or premonitions of that same event on the other. It is like watching something come gradually into focus: first it hangs in the clouds of myth and ritual, vast and vague, then it condenses, grows hard and in a sense small, as a historical event in first century Palestine. This gradual focussing goes on even inside the Christian tradition itself. The earliest stratum of the Old Testament contains many truths in a form which I take to be legendary, or even mythical—hanging in the clouds: but gradually the truth condenses, becomes more and more historical. From things like Noah's Ark or the sun standing still upon Ajalon, you come down to the court memoirs of King David. Finally you reach the New Testament and history reigns supreme, and the Truth is incarnate. And "incarnate" is here more than a metaphor. It is not an accidental resemblance that what, from the point of view of being, is stated in the form "God became Man", should involve, from the point of view of human knowledge, the statement "Myth became Fact". The essential meaning of all things came down from the "heaven" of myth to the "earth" of history. In so doing, it partly emptied itself of its glory, as Christ emptied Himself of His glory to be Man. That is the real explanation of the fact that Theology, far from defeating its rivals by a superior poetry, is, in a superficial but quite real sense, less poetical than they. That is why the New Testament is, in the same sense, less poetical than the Old. Have you not often felt in Church, if the first lesson is some great passage, that the second lesson is somehow small by comparison—almost, if one might say so, hum-drum? So it is and so it must be. This is the humiliation of myth into fact, of God into Man: what is everywhere and always, imageless and ineffable, only to be glimpsed in dream and symbol and the acted poetry of ritual, becomes small, solid—no bigger than a man who can lie asleep in a rowing boat on the Lake of Galilee. You may say that this, after all, is a still deeper poetry. I will not contradict you. The humiliation leads to a greater glory. But the humiliation of God and the shrinking or condensation of the myth as it becomes fact, are also quite real.

I have just mentioned symbol: and that brings me to the last head under which I will consider the charge of "mere poetry". Theology certainly shares with poetry the use of metaphorical or symbolical language. The first Person of the Trinity is not the Father of the Second in a physical sense. The Second Person did not come "down" to earth in the same sense as a parachutist: nor re-ascend into the sky like a balloon: nor did He literally sit at the right hand of the Father. Why, then, does Christianity talk as if all these things did happen? The agnostic thinks that it does so because those who founded it were quite naïvely ignorant and believed all these statements literally; and we later Christians have gone on using the same language through timidity and conservatism. We are often invited, in Professor Price's words, to throw away the shell and retain the kernel.

There are two questions involved here.

1. What did the early Christians believe? Did they believe that God really has a material palace in the sky and that He received His Son in a decorated state chair placed a little to the right of His own?—or did they not? The answer is that the alternative we are offering them was probably never present to their minds at all. As soon as it was present, we know quite well which side of the fence they came down. As soon as the issue of Anthropomorphism was explicitly before the Church in, I think, the second century, Anthropomorphism was condemned. The Church knew the answer (that God has no body and therefore couldn't sit in a chair) as soon as it knew the question. But till the question was raised, of course, people believed neither the one answer nor the other. There is no more tiresome error in the history of thought than to try to sort our ancestors on to this or that side of a distinction which was not in their minds at all. You are asking a question to which no answer exists. It is very probable that most (almost certainly not all) of the first generation of Christians never thought of their faith without anthropomorphic imagery: and that they were not explicitly conscious, as a modern would be, that it *was* mere imagery. But this does not in the least mean that the essence of their belief was concerned with details about a celestial throne room. That was not what they valued, or what they were prepared to die for. Any one of them who went to Alexandria and got a philosophical education would have recognised the imagery at once for what it was, and would not have felt that his belief had been altered in any way that mattered. My mental picture of an Oxford college, before I saw one, was very different from the reality in physical details. But this did not mean that when I came to Oxford I found my general conception of what a college means to have been a delusion. The physical pictures had inevitably accompanied my thinking, but they had never been what I was chiefly interested in, and much of my thinking had been correct in spite of them. What you think is

one thing: what you imagine while you are thinking is another.

The earliest Christians were not so much like a man who mistakes the shell for the kernel as like a man carrying a nut which he hasn't yet cracked. The moment it is cracked, he knows which part to throw away. Till then he holds on to the nut: not because he is a fool but because he isn't.

2. We are invited to restate our belief in a form free from metaphor and symbol. The reason why we don't is that we can't. We can, if you like, say "God entered history" instead of saying "God came down to earth". But, of course, "entered" is just as metaphorical as "came down". You have only substituted horizontal or undefined movement for vertical movement. We can make our language duller; we cannot make it less metaphorical. We can make the pictures more prosaic; we cannot be less pictorial. Nor are we Christians alone in this disability. Here is a sentence from a celebrated anti-Christian writer, Dr. I. A. Richards.[1] "Only that part of the course of a mental event which takes effect through incoming (sensory) impulses or through effects of past sensory impulses can be said to be thereby known. The reservation no doubt involves complications." Dr. Richards does not mean that the part of the course "takes" effect in the literal sense of the word *takes*, nor that it does so *through* a sensory impulse as you could take a parcel *through* a doorway. In the second sentence "The reservation involves complications", he does not mean that an act of defending, or a seat booked in a train, or an American park, really sets about rolling or folding or curling up a set of coilings or rollings up. In other words, all language about things other than physical objects is necessarily metaphorical.

For all these reasons, then, I think (though we knew even before Freud that the heart is deceitful) that those who accept Theology are not necessarily being guided by taste rather than

[1] *Principles of Literary Criticism*, cap. XI.

reason. The picture so often painted of Christians huddling together on an ever narrower strip of beach while the incoming tide of "Science" mounts higher and higher, corresponds to nothing in my own experience. That grand myth which I asked you to admire a few minutes ago is not for me a hostile novelty breaking in on my traditional beliefs. On the contrary, that cosmology is what I started from. Deepening distrust and final abandonment of it long preceded my conversion to Christianity. Long before I believed Theology to be true I had already decided that the popular scientific picture at any rate was false. One absolutely central inconsistency ruins it; it is the one we touched on a fortnight ago. The whole picture professes to depend on inferences from observed facts. Unless inference is valid, the whole picture disappears. Unless we can be sure that reality in the remotest nebula or the remotest part obeys the thought-laws of the human scientist here and now in his laboratory—in other words, unless Reason is an absolute—all is in ruins. Yet those who ask me to believe this world picture also ask me to believe that Reason is simply the unforeseen and unintended by-product of mindless matter at one stage of its endless and aimless becoming. Here is flat contradiction. They ask me at the same moment to accept a conclusion and to discredit the only testimony on which that conclusion can be based. The difficulty is to me a fatal one; and the fact that when you put it to many scientists, far from having an answer, they seem not even to understand what the difficulty is, assures me that I have not found a mare's nest but detected a radical disease in their whole mode of thought from the very beginning. The man who has once understood the situation is compelled henceforth to regard the scientific cosmology as being, in principle, a myth; though no doubt a great many true particulars have been worked into it.[1]

[1] It is not irrelevant, in considering the mythical character of this cosmology to notice that the two great imaginative expressions of it are *earlier* than the evidence: Keats's *Hyperion* and the *Nibelung's Ring* are pre-Darwinian works.

Is Theology Poetry?

After that it is hardly worth noticing minor difficulties. Yet these are many and serious. The Bergsonian critique of orthodox Darwinism is not easy to answer. More disquieting still is Professor D. M. S. Watson's defence. "Evolution itself," he wrote,[1] "is accepted by zoologists not because it has been observed to occur or . . . can be proved by logically coherent evidence to be true, but because the only alternative, special creation, is clearly incredible." Has it come to that? Does the whole vast structure of modern naturalism depend not on positive evidence but simply on an *a priori* metaphysical prejudice? Was it devised not to get in facts but to keep out God? Even, however, if Evolution in the strict biological sense has some better grounds than Professor Watson suggests—and I can't help thinking it must—we should distinguish Evolution in this strict sense from what may be called the universal evolutionism of modern thought. By universal evolutionism I mean the belief that the very formula of universal process is from imperfect to perfect, from small beginnings to great endings, from the rudimentary to the elaborate: the belief which makes people find it natural to think that morality springs from savage taboos, adult sentiment from infantile sexual maladjustments, thought from instinct, mind from matter, organic from inorganic, cosmos from chaos. This is perhaps the deepest habit of mind in the contemporary world. It seems to me immensely unplausible, because it makes the general course of nature so very unlike those parts of nature we can observe. You remember the old puzzle as to whether the owl came from the egg or the egg from the owl. The modern acquiescence in universal evolutionism is a kind of optical illusion, produced by attending exclusively to the owl's emergence from the egg. We are taught from childhood to notice how the perfect oak grows from the acorn and to forget that the acorn itself was dropped by a perfect oak. We are reminded constantly that the adult human

[1] Quoted in *Science and the B.B.C.*, *Nineteenth Century*, April, 1943.

being was an embryo, never that the life of the embryo came from two adult human beings. We love to notice that the express engine of today is the descendant of the "Rocket"; we do not equally remember that the "Rocket" springs not from some even more rudimentary engine, but from something much more perfect and complicated than itself—namely, a man of genius. The obviousness or naturalness which most people seem to find in the idea of emergent evolution thus seems to be a pure hallucination.

On these grounds and others like them one is driven to think that whatever else may be true, the popular scientific cosmology at any rate is certainly not. I left that ship not at the call of poetry but because I thought it could not keep afloat. Something like philosophical idealism or Theism must, at the very worst, be less untrue than that. And idealism turned out, when you took it seriously, to be disguised Theism. And once you accepted Theism you could not ignore the claims of Christ. And when you examined them it appeared to me that you could adopt no middle position. Either he was a lunatic, or God. And He was not a lunatic.

I was taught at school, when I had done a sum, to "prove my answer". The proof or verification of my Christian answer to the cosmic sum is this. When I accept Theology I may find difficulties, at this point or that, in harmonising it with some particular truths which are imbedded in the mythical cosmology derived from science. But I can get in, or allow for, science as a whole. Granted that Reason is prior to matter and that the light of that primal Reason illuminates finite minds, I can understand how men should come, by observation and inference, to know a lot about the universe they live in. If, on the other hand, I swallow the scientific cosmology as a whole, then not only can I not fit in Christianity, but I cannot even fit in science. If minds are wholly dependent on brains, and brains on bio-chemistry, and biochemistry (in the long run) on the meaningless flux of the atoms, I cannot understand how the thought of those minds should have any more significance than the sound of the wind in the trees. And this is to me the final test. This is how I distinguish dreaming and waking. When I am awake I can, in some degree, account for and study my dream. The dragon that pursued me last night can be fitted into my waking world. I know that there are such things as dreams: I know that I had eaten an indigestible dinner: I know that a man of my reading might be expected to dream of dragons. But while in the nightmare I could not have fitted in my waking experience. The waking world is judged more real because it can thus contain the dreaming world; the dreaming world is judged less real because it cannot contain the waking one. For the same reason I am certain that in passing from the scientific point of view to the theological, I have passed from dream to waking. Christian theology can fit in science, art, morality, and the sub-Christian religions. The scientific point of view cannot fit in any of these things, not even science itself. I believe in Christianity as I believe that the Sun has risen not only because I see it but because by it I see everything else.

The Oxford Socratic Club, 1944

10

Transposition

IN THE church to which I belong this day is set apart for commemorating the descent of the Holy Ghost upon the first Christians shortly after the Ascension. I want to consider one of the phenomena which accompanied, or followed, this descent; the phenomenon which our translation calls "speaking with tongues" and which the learned call *glossolalia*. You will not suppose that I think this the most important aspect of Pentecost, but I have two reasons for selecting it. In the first place it would be ridiculous for me to speak about the nature of the Holy Ghost or the modes of His operation: that would be an attempt to teach when I have nearly all to learn. In the second place, *glossolalia* has often been a stumbling-block to me. It is, to be frank, an embarrassing phenomenon. St. Paul himself seems to have been rather embarrassed by it in 1 Corinthians and labours to turn the desire and the attention of the Church to more obviously edifying gifts. But he goes no further. He throws in almost parenthetically the statement that he himself spoke with tongues more than anyone else, and he does not question the spiritual, or supernatural, source of the phenomenon.

The difficulty I feel is this. On the one hand, *glossolalia* has remained an intermittent "variety of religious experience" down to the present day. Every now and then we hear that in some revivalist meeting one or more of those present has burst into a torrent of what appears to be gibberish. The thing does not seem to be edifying, and all non-Christian opinion would regard it as a kind of hysteria, an involuntary discharge of nervous excitement. A good deal even of Christian opinion would explain most instances of it in exactly the same way; and I must confess that it would be very hard to believe that in all instances of it the Holy Ghost is operating. We suspect, even if we cannot be sure, that it is usually an affair of the nerves. That is one horn of the dilemma. On the other hand, we cannot as Christians shelve the story of Pentecost or deny that there, at any rate, the speaking with tongues was miraculous. For the men spoke not gibberish but languages unknown to them though known to other people present. And the whole event of which this makes part is built into the very fabric of the birth-story of the Church. It is this very event which the risen Lord had told the Church to wait for —almost in the last words He uttered before His ascension. It looks, therefore, as if we shall have to say that the very same phenomenon which is sometimes not only natural but even pathological is at other times (or at least at one other time) the organ of the Holy Ghost. And this seems at first very surprising and very open to attack. The sceptic will certainly seize this opportunity to talk to us about Occam's razor, to accuse us of multiplying hypotheses. If most instances of *glossolalia* are covered by hysteria, is it not (he will ask) extremely probable that that explanation covers the remaining instances too?

It is to this difficulty that I would gladly bring a little ease if I can. And I will begin by pointing out that it belongs to a class of difficulties. The closest parallel to it within that class is raised by the erotic language and imagery we find in the mystics. In them we find a whole range of expressions—and therefore possibly of emotions—with which we are quite familiar in another context and which, in that other context, have a clear natural significance. But in the mystical writings it is claimed that these elements have a different cause. And once more the sceptic will ask why the cause which we are content to accept for ninety-nine instances of such language should not be held to cover the hundredth too. The hypothesis that mysticism is an erotic phenomenon will seem to him immensely more probable than any other.

Put in its most general terms our problem is that of the obvious continuity between things which are admittedly natural and things which, it is claimed, are spiritual; the reappearance in what professes to be our supernatural life of all the same old elements which make up our natural life and (it would seem) of no others. If we have really been visited by a revelation from beyond Nature, is it not very strange that an Apocalypse can furnish heaven with nothing more than selections from terrestrial experience (crowns, thrones, and music), that devotion can find no language but that of human lovers, and that the rite whereby Christians enact a mystical union should turn out to be only the old, familiar act of eating and drinking? And you may add that the very same problem also breaks out on a lower level, not only between spiritual and natural but also between higher and lower levels of the natural life. Hence cynics very plausibly challenge our civilised conception of the difference between love and lust by pointing out that when all is said and done they usually end in what is, physically, the same act. They similarly challenge the difference between justice and revenge on the ground that what finally happens to the criminal may be the same. And in all these cases, let us admit that the cynics and sceptics have a good *prima facie* case. The same acts do reappear in justice as well as in revenge : the consummation of humanised and conjugal love is physiologically the same as that of the merely biological lust; religious language and imagery, and probably religious emotion too, contains nothing that has not been borrowed from Nature.

Now it seems to me that the only way to refute the critic here is to show that the same *prima facie* case is equally plausible in some instance where we all know (not by faith or by logic, but empirically) that it is in fact false. Can we find an instance of higher and lower where the higher is within almost everyone's experience? I think we can. Consider the following quotation from *Pepys's Diary*:

With my wife to the King's House to see *The Virgin Martyr*, and it is mighty pleasant. . . . But that which did please me beyond anything in the whole world was the wind musick when the angel comes down, which is so sweet that it ravished me and, indeed, in a word, did wrap up my soul so that it made me really sick, just as I have formerly been when in love with my wife . . . and makes me resolve to practise wind musick and to make my wife do the like. (27th February, 1668.)

There are several points here that deserve attention. Firstly that the internal sensation accompanying intense aesthetic delight was indistinguishable from the sensation accompanying two other experiences, that of being in love and that of being, say, in a rough channel crossing. (2) That of these two other experiences one at least is the very reverse of pleasurable. No man enjoys nausea. (3) That Pepys was, nevertheless, anxious to have again the experience whose sensational accompaniment was identical with the very unpleasant accompaniments of sickness. That was why he decided to take up wind music.

Now it may be true that not many of us have fully shared Pepys's experience; but we have all experienced that sort of thing. For myself I find that if, during a moment of intense aesthetic rapture, one tries to turn round and catch by introspection what one is actually feeling, one can never lay one's hand on anything but a physical sensation. In my case it is a kind of kick or flutter in the diaphragm. Perhaps that is all Pepys meant by "really sick". But the important point is this: I find that this kick or flutter is exactly the same sensation which, in me, accompanies great and sudden anguish. Introspection can discover no difference at all between my neural response to very bad news and my neural response to the overture of *The Magic Flute*. If I were to judge simply by sensations I should come to the absurd conclusion that joy and anguish are the same thing, that what I most dread is the same with what I most desire. Introspection discovers nothing more or different in the one than in the other. And I expect that most of you, if you are in the habit of noticing such things, will report more or less the same.

Now let us take a step farther. These sensations—Pepys's sickness and my flutter in the diaphragm—do not merely accompany very different experiences as an irrelevant or neutral addition. We may be quite sure that Pepys hated that sensation when it came in real sickness: and we know from his own words that he liked it when it came with wind music, for he took measures to make as sure as possible of getting it again. And I likewise love this internal flutter in one context and call it a pleasure and hate it in another and call it misery. It is not a mere sign of joy and anguish: it becomes what it signifies. When the joy thus flows over into the nerves, that overflow is its consummation: when the anguish thus flows over, that physical symptom is the crowning horror. The very same thing which makes the sweetest drop of all in the sweet cup also makes the bitterest drop in the bitter.

And here, I suggest, we have found what we are looking for. I take our emotional life to be "higher" than the life of our sensations—not, of course, morally higher, but richer, more varied, more subtle. And this is a higher level which nearly all of us know. And I believe that if anyone watches carefully the relation between his emotions and his sensations he will discover the following facts; (1) that the nerves do respond, and in a sense most adequately and exquisitely, to the emotions; (2) that their resources are far more limited, the possible variations of sense far fewer, than those of emotion; (3) and that the senses compensate for this by using the *same* sensation to express more than one emotion—even, as we have seen, to express opposite emotions.

Transposition

Where we tend to go wrong is in assuming that if there is to be a correspondence between two systems it must be a one for one correspondence—that A in the one system must be represened by *a* in the other, and so on. But the correspondence between emotion and sensation turns out not to be of that sort. And there never could be correspondence of that sort where the one system was really richer than the other. If the richer system is to be represented in the poorer at all, this can only be by giving each element in the poorer system more than one meaning. The transposition of the richer into the poorer must, so to speak, be algebraical, not arithmetical. If you are to translate from a language which has a large vocabulary into a language that has a small vocabulary, then you must be allowed to use several words in more than one sense. If you are to write a language with twenty-two vowel sounds in an alphabet with only five vowel characters then you must be allowed to give each of those five characters more than one value. If you are making a piano version of a piece originally scored for an orchestra, then the same piano notes which represent flutes in one passage must also represent violins in another.

As the examples show we are all quite familiar with this kind of transposition or adaptation from a richer to a poorer medium. The most familiar example of all is the art of drawing. The problem here is to represent a three-dimensional world on a flat sheet of paper. The solution is perspective, and perspective means that we must give more than one value to a two-dimensional shape. Thus in a drawing of a cube we use an acute angle to represent what is a right angle in the real world. But elsewhere an acute angle on the paper may represent what was already an acute angle in the real world: for example, the point of a spear or the gable of a house. The very same shape which you must draw to give the illusion of a straight road receding from the spectator is also the shape you draw for a dunce's cap. As with the lines, so with the shading. Your brightest light in the picture is, in literal fact, only plain white paper: and this must do for the sun, or a lake in evening light, or snow, or human flesh.

I now make two comments on the instances of Transposition which are already before us:

(1) It is clear that in each case what is happening in the lower medium can be understood only if we know the higher medium. The instance where this knowledge is most commonly lacking is the musical one. The piano version means one thing to the musician who knows the original orchestral score and another thing to the man who hears it simply as a piano piece. But the second man would be at an even greater disadvantage if he had never heard any instrument but a piano and even doubted the existence of other instruments. Even more, we understand pictures only because we know and inhabit the three-dimensional world. If we can imagine a creature who perceived only two dimensions and yet could somehow be aware of the lines as he crawled over them on the paper, we shall easily see how impossible it would be for him to understand. At first he might be prepared to accept on authority our assurance that there was a world in three dimensions. But when we pointed to the lines on the paper and tried to explain, say, that "This is a road", would he not reply that the shape which we were asking him to accept as a revelation of our mysterious other world was the very same shape which, on our own showing, elsewhere meant nothing but a triangle. And soon, I think, he would say, "You keep on telling me of this other world and its unimaginable shapes which you call solid. But isn't it very suspicious that all the shapes which you offer me as images or reflections of the solid ones turn out on inspection to be simply the old two-dimensional shapes of my own world as I have always known it? Is it not obvious that your vaunted other world, so far from being the archetype, is a dream which borrows all its elements from this one?"

(2) It is of some importance to notice that the word *symbolism* is not adequate in all cases to cover the relation between the higher medium and its transposition in the lower. It covers some cases perfectly, but not others. Thus the relation between speech and writing is one of symbolism. The written characters exist solely for the eye, the spoken words solely for the ear. There is complete discontinuity between them. They are not like one another, nor does the one cause the other to be. The one is simply a *sign* of the other and signifies it by a convention. But a picture is not related to the visible world in just that way. Pictures are part of the visible world themselves and represent it only by being part of it. Their visibility has the same source. The suns and lamps in pictures seem to shine only because real suns or lamps shine on them: that is, they seem to shine a great deal because they really shine a little in reflecting their archetypes. The sunlight in a picture is therefore not related to real sunlight simply as written words are to spoken. It is a sign, but also something more than a sign: and only a sign because it is also more than a sign, because in it the thing signified is really in a certain mode present. If I had to name the relation I should call it not symbolical but sacramental. But in the case we started from—that of emotion and sensation—we are even further beyond mere symbolism. For there, as we have seen, the very same sensation does not merely accompany, nor merely signify, diverse and opposite emotions, but becomes part of them. The emotion descends bodily, as it were, into the sensation and digests, transforms, transubstantiates it, so that the same thrill along the nerves *is* delight or *is* agony.

I am not going to maintain that what I call Transposition is the only possible mode whereby a poorer medium can respond to a richer: but I claim that it is very hard to imagine any other. It is therefore, at the very least, not improbable that Transposition occurs whenever the higher reproduces itself in the lower. Thus, to digress for a moment, it seems to me very likely that the real relation beween mind and body is one of Transposition. We are certain that, in this life at any rate, thought is intimately connected with the brain. The theory that thought therefore is merely a movement in the brain is, in my opinion, nonsense; for if so, that theory itself would be merely a movement, an event among atoms, which may have speed and direction but of which it would be meaningless to use the words "true" or "false". We are driven then to some kind of correspondence. But if we assume a one-for-one correspondence this means that we have to attribute an almost unbelievable complexity and variety of events to the brain. But I submit that a one-for-one relation is probably quite unnecessary. All our examples suggest that the brain can respond —in a sense, adequately and exquisitely correspond—to the seemingly infinite variety of consciousness without providing one single physical modification for each single modification of consciousness.

But that is a digression. Let us now return to our original question, about Spirit and Nature, God and Man. Our problem was that in what claims to be our spiritual life all the elements of our natural life recur: and, what is worse, it looks at first glance as if no other elements were present. We now see that if the spiritual is richer than the natural (as no one who believes in its existence would deny) then this is exactly what we should expect. And the sceptic's conclusion that the so-called spiritual is really derived from the natural, that it is a mirage or projection or imaginary extension of the natural, is also exactly what we should expect; for, as we have seen, this is the mistake which an observer who knew only the lower medium would be bound to make in every case of Transposition. The brutal man never can by analysis find anything but lust in love; the Flatlander never can find anything but flat shapes in a picture; physiology never can find anything in thought except twitchings of the grey matter. It is no good browbeating the critic who approaches a Transposition from below. On the evidence available to him his conclusion is the only one possible.

Everything is different when you approach the Transposition from above, as we all do in the case of emotion and sensation or of the three-dimensional world and pictures, and as the spiritual man does in the case we are considering. Those who spoke with tongues, as St. Paul did, can well understand how that holy phenomenon differed from the hysterical phenomenon—although be it remembered, they were in a sense exactly the same phenomenon, just as the very same sensation came to Pepys in love, in the enjoyment of music, and in sickness. Spiritual things are spiritually discerned. The spiritual man judges all things and is judged of none.

But who dares claim to be a spiritual man? In the full sense, none of us. And yet we are somehow aware that we approach from above, or from inside, at least some of those Transpositions which embody the Christian life in this world. With whatever sense of unworthiness, with whatever sense of audacity, we must affirm that we know a little of the higher system which is being transposed. In a way the claim we are making is not a very startling one. We are only claiming to know that our apparent devotion, whatever else it may have been, was not simply erotic, or that our apparent desire for Heaven, whatever else it may have been, was not simply a desire for longevity or jewellery or social splendours. Perhaps we have never really attained at all to what St. Paul would describe as spiritual life. But at the very least we know, in some dim and confused way, that we were trying to use natural acts and images and language with a new value, have at least desired a repentance which was not merely prudential and a love which was not self-centred. At the worst, we know enough of the spiritual to know that we have fallen short of it: as if the picture knew enough of the three-dimensional world to be aware that it was flat.

It is not only for humility's sake (that, of course) that we must emphasise the dimness of our knowledge. I suspect that, save by God's direct miracle, spiritual experience can never abide introspection. If even our emotions will not do so (since the attempt to find out what we are now *feeling* yields nothing more than a physical sensation), much less will the operations of the Holy Ghost. The attempt to discover by introspective analysis our own spiritual condition is to me a horrible thing which reveals, at best, not the secrets of God's spirit and ours, but their transpositions in intellect, emotion and imagination, and which at worst may be the quickest road to presumption or despair.

I believe that this doctrine of Transposition provides for most of us a background very much needed for the theological virtue of Hope. We can hope only for what we can desire. And the trouble is that any adult and philosophically respectable notion we can form of Heaven is forced to deny of that state most of the things our nature desires. There is no doubt a blessedly ingenuous faith, a child's or a savage's faith which finds no difficulty. It accepts without awkward questionings the harps and golden streets and the family reunions pictured by hymn-writers. Such a faith is deceived, yet, in the deepest sense, not deceived; for while it errs in mistaking symbol for fact, yet it apprehends Heaven as joy and plenitude and love. But it is impossible for most of us. And we must not try, by artifice, to make ourselves more naïf than we are. A man does not "become as a little child" by aping childhood. Hence our notion of Heaven involves perpetual negations; no food, no drink, no sex, no movement, no mirth, no events, no time, no art.

Against all these, to be sure, we set one positive: the vision and enjoyment of God. And since this is an infinite good we hold (rightly) that it outweighs them all. That is, the reality of the Beatific Vision would, or will, outweigh, would infinitely outweigh, the reality of the negations. But can our present notion of it outweigh our present notion of them? That is quite a different question. And for most of us at most times the answer is No. How it may be for great saints and mystics I cannot tell. But for others the conception of that Vision is a difficult, precarious and fugitive extrapolation from a very few and ambiguous moments in our earthly experience: while our idea of the negated natural goods is vivid and persistent, loaded with the memories of a lifetime, built into our nerves and muscles and therefore into our imaginations.

Thus the negatives have, so to speak, an unfair advantage in every competition with the positive. What is worse, their presence —and most when we most resolutely try to suppress or ignore them—vitiates even such a faint and ghostlike notion of the positive as we might have had. The exclusion of the lower goods begins to seem the essential characteristic of the higher good. We feel, if we do not say, that the vision of God will come not to fulfil but to destroy our nature; this bleak fantasy often underlies our very use of such words as "holy" or "pure" or "spiritual".

We must not allow this to happen if we can possibly prevent it. We must believe—and therefore in some degree imagine—that every negation will be only the reverse side of a fulfilling. And we must mean by that the fulfilling, precisely, of our humanity; not our transformation into angels nor our absorption into Deity. For though we shall be "as the angels" and made "like unto" our Master, I think this means "like with the likeness proper to men": as different instruments that play the same air but each in its own fashion. How far the life of the risen man will be sensory, we do not know. But I surmise that it will differ from the sensory life we know here, not as emptiness differs from water or water from wine but as a flower differs from a bulb or a cathedral from an architect's drawing. And it is here that Transposition helps me.

Let us construct a fable. Let us picture a woman thrown into a dungeon. There she bears and rears a son. He grows up seeing nothing but the dungeon walls, the straw on the floor, and a little patch of the sky seen through the grating, which is too high up to show anything except sky. This unfortunate woman was an artist, and when they imprisoned her she managed to bring with her a drawing pad and a box of pencils. As she never loses the hope of deliverance she is constantly teaching her son about that outer world which he has never seen. She does it very largely by drawing him pictures. With her pencil she attempts to show him what fields, rivers, mountains, cities and waves on a beach are like. He is a dutiful boy and he does his best to believe her when she tells him that that outer world is far more interesting and glorious than anything in the dungeon. At times he succeeds. On the whole he gets on tolerably well until, one day, he says something that gives his mother pause. For a minute or two they are at cross-purposes. Finally it dawns on her that he has, all these years, lived under a misconception. "But", she gasps, "you didn't think that the real world was full of lines drawn in lead pencil?" "What?" says the boy. "No pencil-marks there?" And instantly his whole notion of the outer world becomes a blank. For the lines, by which alone he was imagining it, have now been denied of it. He has no idea of that which will exclude and dispense with the lines, that of which the lines were merely a transposition —the waving tree-tops, the light dancing on the weir, the coloured three-dimensional realities which are not enclosed in lines but define their own shapes at every moment with a delicacy and multiplicity which no drawing could ever achieve. The child will get the idea that the real world is somehow less visible than his mother's pictures. In reality it lacks lines because it is incomparably more visible.

So with us. "We know not what we shall be"; but we may be sure we shall be more, not less, than we were on earth. Our natural experiences (sensory, emotional, imaginative) are only like the drawing, like pencilled lines on flat paper. If they vanish in the risen life, they will vanish only as pencil lines vanish from the real landscape; not as a candle flame that is put out but as a candle flame which becomes invisible because someone has pulled up the blind, thrown open the shutters, and let in the blaze of the risen sun.

You can put it whichever way you please. You can say that by Transposition our humanity, senses and all, can be made the vehicle of beatitude. Or you can say that the heavenly bounties by Transposition are embodied during this life in our temporal experience. But the second way is the better. It is the present life which is the diminution, the symbol, the etiolated, the (as it were) "vegetarian" substitute. If flesh and blood cannot inherit the Kingdom, that is not because they are too solid, too gross, too distinct, too "illustrious with being". They are too flimsy, too transitory, too phantasmal.

With this my case, as the lawyers say, is complete. But I have just four points to add:

1. I hope it is quite clear that the conception of Transposition, as I call it, is distinct from another conception often used for the same purpose—I mean the conception of development. The Developmentalist explains the continuity between things that claim to be spiritual and things that are certainly natural by saying that the one slowly turned into the other. I believe this view explains some facts, but I think it has been much overworked. At any rate it is not the theory I am putting forward. I am not saying that the natural act of eating after millions of years somehow blossoms into the Christian sacrament. I am saying that the Spiritual Reality, which existed before there were any creatures who ate, gives this natural act a new meaning, and more than a new meaning: makes it in a certain context to be a different thing. In a word, I think that real landscapes enter into pictures, not that pictures will one day sprout out into real trees and grass.

2. I have found it impossible, in thinking of what I call Transposition, not to ask myself whether it may help us to conceive the Incarnation. Of course if Transposition were merely a mode of symbolism it could give us no help at all in this matter: on the contrary, it would lead us wholly astray, back into a new kind of Docetism (or would it be only the old kind?) and away from the utterly historical and concrete reality which is the centre of all our hope, faith and love. But then, as I have pointed out, Transposition is not always symbolism. In varying degrees the lower reality can actually be drawn into the higher and become part of it. The sensation which accompanies joy becomes itself joy: we can hardly choose but say "incarnates joy". If this is so, then I venture to suggest, though with great doubt and in the most provisional way, that the concept of Transposition may have some contribution to make to the theology—or at least to the philosophy—of the Incarnation. For we are told in one of the creeds that the Incarnation worked "not by conversion of the Godhead into flesh, but by taking of the Manhood into God". And it seems to me that there is a real analogy between this and what I have called Transposition: that humanity, still remaining itself, is not merely counted as, but veritably drawn into, Deity, seems to me like what happens when a sensation (not in itself a pleasure) is drawn into the joy it accompanies. But I walk *in mirabilibus supra me* and submit all to the verdict of real theologians.

3. I have tried to stress throughout the inevitableness of the error made about every transposition by one who approaches it from the lower medium only. The strength of such a critic lies in the words "merely" or "nothing but". He sees all the facts but not the meaning. Quite truly, therefore, he claims to have seen all the facts. There *is* nothing else there; except the meaning. He is therefore, as regards the matter in hand, in the position of an animal. You will have noticed that most dogs cannot understand *pointing*. You point to a bit of food on the floor: the dog, instead

of looking at the floor, sniffs at your finger. A finger is a finger to him, and that is all. His world is all fact and no meaning. And in a period when factual realism is dominant we shall find people deliberately inducing upon themselves this dog-like mind. A man who has experienced love from within will deliberately go about to inspect it analytically from outside and regard the results of this analysis as truer than his experience. The extreme limit of this self-blinding is seen in those who, like the rest of us, have consciousness, yet go about to study the human organism as if they did not know it was conscious. As long as this deliberate refusal to understand things from above, even where such understanding is possible, continues, it is idle to talk of any final victory over materialism. The critique of every experience from below, the voluntary ignoring of meaning and concentration on fact, will always have the same plausibility. There will always be evidence, and every month fresh evidence, to show that religion is only psychological, justice only self-protection, politics only economics, love only lust, and thought itself only cerebral biochemistry.

4. Finally, I suggest that what has been said of Transposition throws a new light on the doctrine of the resurrection of the body. For in a sense Transposition can do anything. However great the difference between Spirit and Nature, between aesthetic joy and that flutter in the diaphragm, between reality and picture, yet the Transposition can be in its own way adequate. I said before that in your drawing you had only plain white paper for sun and cloud, snow, water, and human flesh. In one sense, how miserably inadequate! Yet in another, how perfect. If the shadows are properly done, that patch of white paper will, in some curious way, be very like blazing sunshine: we shall almost feel cold while we look at the paper snow and almost warm our hands at the paper fire. May we not, by a reasonable analogy, suppose likewise that there is no experience of the spirit so transcendent and supernatural, no vision of Deity Himself so close and so far

beyond all images and emotions, that to it also there cannot be an appropriate correspondence on the sensory level? Not by a new sense but by the incredible flooding of those very sensations we now have with a meaning, a transvaluation, of which we have here no faintest guess?

A Sermon at Mansfield College, Oxford

11

On Obstinacy in Belief

PAPERS HAVE more than once been read to the Socratic Club at Oxford in which a contrast was drawn between a supposedly Christian attitude and a supposedly scientific attitude to belief. We have been told that the scientist thinks it his duty to proportion the strength of his belief exactly to the evidence; to believe less as there is less evidence and to withdraw belief altogether when reliable adverse evidence turns up. We have been told that, on the contrary, the Christian regards it as positively praiseworthy to believe without evidence, or in excess of the evidence, or to maintain his belief unmodified in the teeth of steadily increasing evidence against it. Thus a "faith that has stood firm", which appears to mean a belief immune from all the assaults of reality, is commended.

If this were a fair statement of the case, then the co-existence within the same species of such scientists and such Christians, would be a very staggering phenomenon. The fact that the two classes appear to overlap, as they do, would be quite inexplicable. Certainly all discussion between creatures so different would be hopeless. The purpose of this essay is to show that things are really not quite so bad as that. The sense in which scientists proportion their belief to the evidence and the sense in which Christians do not, both need to be defined more closely. My hope is that when this has been done, though disagreement between the two parties may remain, they will not be left staring at one another in wholly dumb and desperate incomprehension.

And first, a word about belief in general. I do not see that the

183

state of "proportioning belief to evidence" is anything like so common in the scientific life as has been claimed. Scientists are mainly concerned not with believing things but with finding things out. And no one, to the best of my knowledge, uses the word "believe" about things he has found out. The doctor says he "believes" a man was poisoned before he has examined the body; after the examination, he says the man was poisoned. No one says that he believes the multiplication table. No one who catches a thief red-handed says he believes that man was stealing. The scientist, when at work, that is, when he is a scientist, is labouring to escape from belief and unbelief into knowledge. Of course he uses hypotheses or supposals. I do not think these are beliefs. We must look, then, for the scientist's behaviour about belief not to his scientific life but to his leisure hours.

In actual modern English usage the verb "believes", except for two special usages, generally expresses a very weak degree of opinion. "Where is Tom?" "Gone to London, I believe." The speaker would be only mildly surprised if Tom had not gone to London after all. "What was the date?" "430 B.C., I believe." The speaker means that he is far from sure. It is the same with the negative if it is put in the form "I believe not". ("Is Jones coming up this term?" "I believe not.") But if the negative is put in a different form it then becomes one of the special usages I mentioned a moment ago. This is of course the form "I don't believe it", or the still stronger "I don't believe you". "I don't believe it" is far stronger on the negative side than "I believe" is on the positive. "Where is Mrs. Jones?" "Eloped with the butler, I believe." "I don't believe it." This, especially if said with anger, may imply a conviction which in subjective certitude might be hard to distinguish from knowledge by experience. The other special usage is "I believe" as uttered by a Christian. There is no great difficulty in making the hardened materialist understand, however little he approves, the sort of mental attitude which this "I believe" expresses. The materialist need only picture himself replying, to some report of a miracle, "I don't believe it", and then imagine this same degree of conviction on the opposite side. He knows that he cannot, there and then, produce a refutation of the miracle which would have the certainty of mathematical demonstration; but the formal possibility that the miracle might after all have occurred does not really trouble him any more than a fear that water might not be H and O. Similarly, the Christian does not necessarily claim to have demonstrative proof; but the formal possibility that God might not exist is not necessarily present in the form of the least actual doubt. Of course there are Christians who hold that such demonstrative proof exists, just as there may be materialists who hold that there is demonstrative disproof. But then, whichever of them is right (if either is) while he retained the proof or disproof would be not believing or disbelieving but knowing. We are speaking of belief and disbelief in the strongest degree but not of knowledge. Belief, in this sense, seems to me to be assent to a proposition which we think so overwhelmingly probable that there is a psychological exclusion of doubt, though not a logical exclusion of dispute.

It may be asked whether belief (and of course disbelief) of this sort ever attaches to any but theological propositions. I think that many beliefs approximate to it; that is, many probabilities seem to us so strong that the absence of logical certainty does not induce in us the least shade of doubt. The scientific beliefs of those who are not themselves scientists often have this character, especially among the uneducated. Most of our beliefs about other people are of the same sort. The scientist himself, or he who was a scientist in the laboratory, has beliefs about his wife and friends which he holds, not indeed without evidence, but with more certitude than the evidence, if weighed in the laboratory manner, would justify. Most of my generation had a belief in the reality

185

of the external world and of other people—if you prefer it, a disbelief in solipsism—far in excess of our strongest arguments. It may be true, as they now say, that the whole thing arose from category mistakes and was a pseudo-problem; but then we didn't know that in the twenties. Yet we managed to disbelieve in solipsism all the same.

There is, of course, no question so far of belief without evidence. We must beware of confusion between the way in which a Christian first assents to certain propositions and the way in which he afterwards adheres to them. These must be carefully distinguished. Of the second it is true, in a sense, to say that Christians do recommend a certain discounting of apparent contrary evidence, and I will later attempt to explain why. But so far as I know it is not expected that a man should assent to these propositions in the first place without evidence or in the teeth of the evidence. At any rate, if anyone expects that, I certainly do not. And in fact, the man who accepts Christianity always thinks he had good evidence; whether, like Dante, *fisici e metafisici argomenti,* or historical evidence, or the evidence of religious experience, or authority, or all these together. For of course authority, however we may value it in this or that particular instance, is a kind of evidence. All of our historical beliefs, most of our geographical beliefs, many of our beliefs about matters that concern us in daily life, are accepted on the authority of other human beings, whether we are Christians, Atheists, Scientists, or Men-in-the-Street.

It is not the purpose of this essay to weigh the evidence, of whatever kind, on which Christians base their belief. To do that would be to write a full-dress *apologia.* All that I need do here is to point out that, at the very worst, this evidence cannot be so weak as to warrant the view that all whom it convinces are indifferent to evidence. The history of thought seems to make this quite plain. We know, in fact, that believers are not cut off from unbelievers by any portentous inferiority of intelligence or any perverse refusal to think. Many of them have been people of powerful minds. Many of them have been scientists. We may suppose them to have been mistaken, but we must suppose that their error was at least plausible. We might indeed, conclude that it was, merely from the multitude and diversity of the arguments against it. For there is not one case against religion, but many. Some say, like Capaneus in Statius, that it is a projection of our primitive fears, *primus in orbe deos fecit timor*: others, with Euhemerus, that it is all a "plant" put up by wicked kings, priests, or capitalists; others, with Tylor, that it comes from dreams about the dead; others, with Frazer, that it is a by-product of agriculture; others, like Freud, that it is a complex; the moderns that it is a category mistake. I will never believe that an error against which so many and various defensive weapons have been found necessary was, from the outset, wholly lacking in plausibility. All this "post haste and rummage in the land" obviously implies a respectable enemy.

There are of course people in our own day to whom the whole situation seems altered by the doctrine of the concealed wish. They will admit that men, otherwise apparently rational, have been deceived by the arguments for religion. But they will say that they have been deceived first by their own desires and produced the arguments afterwards as a rationalisation: that these arguments have never been intrinsically even plausible, but have seemed so because they were secretly weighted by our wishes. Now I do not doubt that this sort of thing happens in thinking about religion as in thinking about other things: but as a general explanation of religious assent it seems to me quite useless. On that issue our wishes may favour either side or both. The assumption that every man would be pleased, and nothing but pleased, if only he could conclude that Christianity is true, appears to me to be simply preposterous. If Freud is right about the Oedipus complex, the universal pressure of the wish that God should not exist must be enormous, and atheism must be an admirable gratification to one of our strongest suppressed impulses. This argument, in fact, could be used on the theistic side. But I have no intention of so using it. It will not really help either party. It is fatally ambivalent. Men wish on both sides: and again, there is fear-fulfilment as well as wish-fulfilment, and hypochondriac temperaments will always tend to think true what they most wish to be false. Thus instead of the one predicament on which our opponents sometimes concentrate there are in fact four. A man may be a Christian because he wants Christianity to be true. He may be an atheist because he wants atheism to be true. He may be an atheist because he wants Christianity to be true. He may be a Christian because he wants atheism to be true. Surely these possibilities cancel one another out? They may be of some use in analysing a particular instance of belief or disbelief, where we know the case history, but as a general explanation of either they will not help us. I do not think they overthrow the view that there is evidence both for and against the Christian propositions which fully rational minds, working honestly, can assess differently.

I therefore ask you to substitute a different and less tidy picture for that with which we began. In it, you remember, two different kinds of men, scientists, who proportioned their belief to the evidence, and Christians, who did not, were left facing one another across a chasm. The picture I should prefer is like this. All men alike, on questions which interest them, escape from the region of belief into that of knowledge when they can, and if they succeed in knowing, they no longer say they believe. The questions in which mathematicians are interested admit of treatment by a particularly clear and strict technique. Those of the scientist have their own technique, which is not quite the same. Those of the historian and the judge are different again. The mathematician's proof (at least so we laymen suppose) is by reasoning, the scientist's by experiment, the historian's by documents, the judge's by concurring sworn testimony. But all these men, as men, on questions outside their own disciplines, have numerous beliefs to which they do not normally apply the methods of their own disciplines. It would indeed carry some suspicion of morbidity and even of insanity if they did. These beliefs vary in strength from weak opinion to complete subjective certitude. Specimens of such beliefs at their strongest are the Christian's "I believe" and the convinced atheist's "I don't believe a word of it". The particular subject-matter on which these two disagree does not, of course, necessarily involve such strength of belief and disbelief. There are some who moderately opine that there is, or is not, a God. But there are others whose belief or disbelief is free from doubt. And all these beliefs, weak or strong, are based on what appears to the holders to be evidence; but the strong believers or disbelievers of course think they have very strong evidence. There is no need to suppose stark unreason on either side. We need only suppose error. One side has estimated the evidence wrongly. And even so, the mistake cannot be supposed to be of a flagrant nature; otherwise the debate would not continue.

So much, then, for the way in which Christians come to assent to certain propositions. But we have now to consider something quite different; their adherence to their belief after it has once been formed. It is here that the charge of irrationality and resistance to evidence becomes really important. For it must be admitted at once that Christians do praise such an adherence as if it were meritorious; and even, in a sense, more meritorious the stronger the apparent evidence against their faith becomes. They even warn one another that such apparent contrary evidence—such "trials to faith" or "temptations to doubt"—may be expected to occur, and determine in advance to resist them. And this is certainly shockingly unlike the behaviour we all demand of the scientist or the historian in their own disciplines. There, to slur over or ignore the faintest evidence against a favourite hypothesis, is admittedly foolish and shameful. It must be exposed to every test; every doubt must be invited. But then I do not admit that a hypothesis is a belief. And if we consider the scientist not among his hypotheses in the laboratory but among the beliefs in his ordinary life, I think the contrast between him and the Christian would be weakened. If, for the first time, a doubt of his wife's fidelity crosses the scientist's mind, does he consider it his duty at once to entertain this doubt with complete impartiality, at once to evolve a series of experiments by which it can be tested, and to await the result with pure neutrality of mind? No doubt it may come to that in the end. There are unfaithful wives; there are experimental husbands. But is such a course what his brother scientists would recommend to him (all of them, I suppose, except one) as the first step he should take and the only one consistent with his honour as a scientist? Or would they, like us, blame him for a moral flaw rather than praise him for an intellectual virtue if he did so?

This is intended, however, merely as a precaution against exaggerating the difference between Christian obstinacy in belief and the behaviour of normal people about their non-theological beliefs. I am far from suggesting that the case I have supposed is exactly parallel to the Christian obstinacy. For of course evidence of the wife's infidelity might accumulate, and presently reach a point at which the scientist would be pitiably foolish to disbelieve it. But the Christians seem to praise an adherence to the original belief which holds out against any evidence whatever. I must now try to show why such praise is in fact a logical conclusion from the original belief itself.

This can be done best by thinking for a moment of situations in which the thing is reversed. In Christianity such faith is demanded of us; but there are situations in which we demand it of others. There are times when we can do all that a fellow creature needs if only he will trust us. In getting a dog out of a trap, in extracting a thorn from a child's finger, in teaching a boy to swim or rescuing one who can't, in getting a frightened beginner over a nasty place on a mountain, the one fatal obstacle may be their distrust. We are asking them to trust us in the teeth of their senses, their imagination, and their intelligence. We ask them to believe that what is painful will relieve their pain and that what looks dangerous is their only safety. We ask them to accept apparent impossibilities: that moving the paw farther back into the trap is the way to get it out—that hurting the finger very much more will stop the finger hurting—that water which is obviously permeable will resist and support the body—that holding on to the only support within reach is not the way to avoid sinking—that to go higher and on to a more exposed ledge is the way not to fall. To support all these *incredibilia* we can rely only on the other party's confidence in us—a confidence certainly not based on demonstration, admittedly shot through with emotion, and perhaps, if we are strangers, resting on nothing but such assurance as the look of our face and the tone of our voice can supply, or even, for the dog, on our smell. Sometimes, because of their unbelief, we can do no mighty works. But if we succeed, we do so because they have maintained their faith in us against apparently contrary evidence. No one blames us for demanding such faith. No one blames them for giving it. No one says afterwards what an unintelligent dog or child or boy that must have been to trust us. If the young mountaineer were a scientist, it would not be held against him, when he came up for a fellowship, that he had once departed from Clifford's rule of evidence by entertaining a belief with strength greater than the evidence logically obliged him to.

Now to accept the Christian propositions is *ipso facto* to believe that we are to God, always, as that dog or child or bather or mountain climber was to us, only very much more so. From this it is a strictly logical conclusion that the behaviour which was appropriate to them will be appropriate to us, only very much more so. Mark: I am not saying that the strength of our original belief must by psychological necessity produce such behaviour. I am saying that the content of our original belief by logical necessity entails the proposition that such behaviour is appropriate. If human life is in fact ordered by a beneficent being whose knowledge of our real needs and of the way in which they can be satisfied infinitely exceeds our own, we must expect *a priori* that His operations will often appear to us far from beneficent and far from wise, and that it will be our highest prudence to give Him our confidence in spite of this. This expectation is increased by the fact that when we accept Christianity we are warned that apparent evidence against it will occur—evidence strong enough "to deceive if possible the very elect". Our situation is rendered tolerable by two facts. One is that we seem to ourselves, besides the apparently contrary evidence, to receive favourable evidence. Some of it is in the form of external events: as when I go to see a man, moved by what I felt to be a whim, and find he has been praying that I should come to him that day. Some of it is more like the evidence on which the mountaineer or the dog might trust his rescuer—the rescuer's voice, look, and smell. For it seems to us (though you, on your premises, must believe us deluded) that we have something like a knowledge-by-acquaintance of the Person we believe in, however imperfect and intermittent it may be. We trust not because "a God" exists, but because *this* God exists. Or if we ourselves dare not claim to "know" Him, Christendom does, and we trust at least some of its representatives in the same way: because of the sort of people they are. The second fact is this. We think we can see already why, if our original belief is true, such trust beyond the evidence, against much apparent evidence, has to be demanded of us. For the question is not about being helped out of one trap or over one difficult place in a climb. We believe that His intention is to create a certain personal relation between Himself and us, a relation really *sui generis* but analogically describable in terms of filial or of erotic love. Complete trust is an ingredient in that relation—such trust as could have no room to grow except where there is also room for doubt. To love involves trusting the beloved beyond the evidence, even against much evidence. No man is our friend who believes in our good intentions only when they are proved. No man is our friend who will not be very slow to accept evidence against them. Such confidence, between one man and another, is in fact almost universally praised as a moral beauty, not blamed as a logical error. And the suspicious man is blamed for a meanness of character, not admired for the excellence of his logic.

There is, you see, no real parallel between Christian obstinacy in faith and the obstinacy of a bad scientist trying to preserve a hypothesis although the evidence has turned against it. Unbelievers very pardonably get the impression that an adherence to our faith is like that, because they meet Christianity, if at all, mainly in apologetic works. And there, of course, the existence and beneficence of God must appear as a speculative question like any other. Indeed, it is a speculative question as long as it is a question at all. But once it has been answered in the affirmative, you get quite a new situation. To believe that God—at least *this* God—exists is to believe that you as a person now stand in the presence of God as a Person. What would, a moment before, have been variations in opinion, now becomes variations in your personal attitude to a Person. You are no longer faced with an argument which demands your assent, but with a Person who demands your confidence. A faint analogy would be this. It is one thing to discuss *in vacuo* whether So-and-so will join us tonight, and another to discuss this when So-and-So's honour is pledged to come and some great matter depends on his coming. In the first case it would be merely reasonable, as the clock ticked on, to expect him less and less. In the second, a continued expectation far into the night would be due to our friend's character if we had found him reliable before. Which of us would not feel slightly ashamed if one moment after we had given him up he arrived with a full explanation of his delay? We should feel that we ought to have known him better.

Now of course we see, quite as clearly as you, how agonisingly two-edged all this is. A faith of this sort, if it happens to be true, is obviously what we need, and it is infinitely ruinous to lack it. But there can be faith of this sort where it is wholly ungrounded. The dog may lick the face of the man who comes to take it out of the trap; but the man may only mean to vivisect it in South Parks Road when he has done so. The ducks who come to the call "Dilly, dilly, come and be killed" have confidence in the farmer's wife, and she wrings their necks for their pains. There is that famous French story of the fire in the theatre. Panic was spreading, the spectators were just turning from an audience into a mob. At that moment a huge bearded man leaped through the orchestra on to the stage, raised his hand with a gesture full of nobility, and cried, "*Que chacun regagne sa place.*" Such was the authority of his voice and bearing that everyone obeyed him. As a result they were all burned to death, while the bearded man walked quietly out through the wings to the stage door, took a cab which was waiting for someone else, and went home to bed.

That demand for our confidence which a true friend makes of us is exactly the same that a confidence trickster would make. That refusal to trust, which is sensible in reply to a confidence trickster, is ungenerous and ignoble to a friend, and deeply damaging to our relation with him. To be forewarned and therefore forearmed against apparently contrary appearance is eminently rational if our belief is true; but if our belief is a delusion, this same forewarning and forearming would obviously be the method whereby the delusion rendered itself incurable. And yet again, to be aware of these possibilities and still to reject them is clearly the precise mode, and the only mode, in which our personal response to God can establish itself. In that sense the ambiguity is not something that conflicts with faith so much as a condition which makes faith possible. When you are asked for trust you may give it or withhold it; it is senseless to say that you will trust if you are given demonstrative certainty. There would be no room for trust if demonstration were given. When demonstration is given what will be left will be simply the sort of relation which results from having trusted, or not having trusted, before it was given.

The saying "Blessed are those that have not seen and have believed" has nothing to do with our original assent to the Christian propositions. It was not addressed to a philosopher inquiring whether God exists. It was addressed to a man who already believed that, who already had long acquaintance with a particular Person, and evidence that that Person could do very odd things, and who then refused to believe one odd thing more, often predicted by that Person and vouched for by all his closest friends. It is a rebuke not to scepticism in the philosophic sense but to the psychological quality of being "suspicious". It says in effect, "You should have known me better." There are cases between man and man where we should all, in our different way, bless those who have not seen and have believed. Our relation to those who trusted us only after we were proved innocent in court cannot be the same as our relation to those who trusted us all through.

Our opponents, then, have a perfect right to dispute with us about the grounds of our original assent. But they must not accuse us of sheer insanity if, after the assent has been given, our

195

adherence to it is no longer proportioned to every fluctuation of the apparent evidence. They cannot of course be expected to know on what our assurance feeds, and how it revives and is always rising from its ashes. They cannot be expected to see how the *quality* of the object which we think we are beginning to know by acquaintance drives us to the view that if this were a delusion then we should have to say that the universe had produced no real thing of comparable value and that all explanations of the delusion seemed somehow less important than the thing explained. That is knowledge we cannot communicate. But they can see how the assent, of necessity, moves us from the logic of speculative thought into what might perhaps be called the logic of personal relations. What would, up till then, have been variations simply of opinion become variations of conduct by a person to a Person. *Credere Deum esse* turns into *Credere in Deum*. And *Deum* here is this God, the increasingly knowable Lord.

The Oxford Socratic Club, 1955

12

The Weight of Glory

IF YOU asked twenty good men today what they thought the highest of the virtues, nineteen of them would reply, Unselfishness. But if you had asked almost any of the great Christians of old he would have replied, Love. You see what has happened? A negative term has been substituted for a positive, and this is of more than philological importance. The negative idea of Unselfishness carries with it the suggestion not primarily of securing good things for others, but of going without them ourselves, as if our abstinence and not their happiness was the important point. I do not think this is the Christian virtue of Love. The New Testament has lots to say about self-denial, but not about self-denial as an end in itself. We are told to deny ourselves and to take up our crosses in order that we may follow Christ; and nearly every description of what we shall ultimately find if we do so contains an appeal to desire. If there lurks in most modern minds the notion that to desire our own good and earnestly to hope for the enjoyment of it is a bad thing, I submit that this notion has crept in from Kant and the Stoics and is no part of the Christian faith. Indeed, if we consider the unblushing promises of reward and the staggering nature of the rewards promised in the Gospels, it would seem that Our Lord finds our desires, not too strong, but too weak. We are half-hearted creatures, fooling about with drink and sex and ambition when infinite joy is offered us, like an ignorant child who wants to go on making mud pies in a slum because he cannot imagine what is meant by the offer of a holiday at the sea. We are far too easily pleased.

We must not be troubled by unbelievers when they say that this promise of reward makes the Christian life a mercenary affair. There are different kinds of reward. There is the reward which has no natural connection with the things you do to earn it, and is quite foreign to the desires that ought to accompany those things. Money is not the natural reward of love, that is why we call a man mercenary if he marries a woman for the sake of her money. But marriage is the proper reward for a real lover, and he is not mercenary for desiring it. A general who fights well in order to get a peerage is mercenary; a general who fights for victory is not, victory being the proper reward of battle as marriage is the proper reward of love. The proper rewards are not simply tacked on to the activity for which they are given, but are the activity itself in consummation. There is also a third case, which is more complicated. An enjoyment of Greek poetry is certainly a proper, and not a mercenary, reward for learning Greek; but only those who have reached the stage of enjoying Greek poetry can tell from their own experience that this is so. The schoolboy beginning Greek grammar cannot look forward to his adult enjoyment of Sophocles as a lover looks forward to marriage or a general to victory. He has to begin by working for marks, or to escape punishment, or to please his parents, or, at best, in the hope of a future good which he cannot at present imagine or desire. His position, therefore, bears a certain resemblance to that of the mercenary; the reward he is going to get will, in actual fact, be a natural or proper reward, but he will not know that till he has got it. Of course, he gets it gradually; enjoyment creeps in upon the mere drudgery, and nobody could point to a day or an hour when the one ceased and the other began. But it is just in so far as he approaches the reward that he becomes able to desire it for its own sake, indeed, the power of so desiring it is itself a preliminary reward.

The Christian, in relation to heaven, is in much the same

position as this schoolboy. Those who have attained everlasting life in the vision of God doubtless know very well that it is no mere bribe, but the very consummation of their earthly discipleship; but we who have not yet attained it cannot know this in the same way, and cannot even begin to know it at all except by continuing to obey and finding the first reward of our obedience in our increasing power to desire the ultimate reward. Just in proportion as the desire grows, our fear lest it should be a mercenary desire will die away and finally be recognised as an absurdity. But probably this will not, for most of us, happen in a day; poetry replaces grammar, gospel replaces law, longing transforms obedience, as gradually as the tide lifts a grounded ship.

But there is one other important similarity between the schoolboy and ourselves. If he is an imaginative boy he will, quite probably, be revelling in the English poets and romancers suitable to his age some time before he begins to suspect that Greek grammar is going to lead him to more and more enjoyments of this same sort. He may even be neglecting his Greek to read Shelley and Swinburne in secret. In other words, the desire which Greek is really going to gratify already exists in him and is attached to objects which seem to him quite unconnected with Xenophon and the verbs in $\mu\iota$. Now, if we are made for heaven, the desire for our proper place will be already in us, but not yet attached to the true object, and will even appear as the rival of that object. And this, I think, is just what we find. No doubt there is one point in which my analogy of the schoolboy breaks down. The English poetry which he reads when he ought to be doing Greek exercises may be just as good as the Greek poetry to which the exercises are leading him, so that in fixing on Milton instead of journeying on to Aeschylus his desire is not embracing a false object. But our case is very different. If a transtemporal, transfinite good is our real destiny, then any other good on which

199

our desire fixes must be in some degree fallacious, must bear at best only a symbolical relation to what will truly satisfy.

In speaking of this desire for our own far-off country, which we find in ourselves even now, I feel a certain shyness. I am almost committing an indecency. I am trying to rip open the inconsolable secret in each one of you—the secret which hurts so much that you take your revenge on it by calling it names like Nostalgia and Romanticism and Adolescence; the secret also which pierces with such sweetness that when, in very intimate conversation, the mention of it becomes imminent, we grow awkward and affect to laugh at ourselves; the secret we cannot hide and cannot tell, though we desire to do both. We cannot tell it because it is a desire for something that has never actually appeared in our experience. We cannot hide it because our experience is constantly suggesting it, and we betray ourselves like lovers at the mention of a name. Our commonest expedient is to call it beauty and behave as if that had settled the matter. Wordsworth's expedient was to identify it with certain moments in his own past. But all this is a cheat. If Wordsworth had gone back to those moments in the past, he would not have found the thing itself, but only the reminder of it; what he remembered would turn out to be itself a remembering. The books or the music in which we thought the beauty was located will betray us if we trust to them; it was not *in* them, it only came *through* them, and what came through them was longing. These things—the beauty, the memory of our own past—are good images of what we really desire; but if they are mistaken for the thing itself they turn into dumb idols, breaking the hearts of their worshippers. For they are not the thing itself; they are only the scent of a flower we have not found, the echo of a tune we have not heard, news from a country we have never yet visited. Do you think I am trying to weave a spell? Perhaps I am; but remember your fairy tales. Spells are used for breaking enchantments as well as for inducing them. And you and I have need of the strongest spell that can be found to wake us from the evil enchantment of worldliness which has been laid upon us for nearly a hundred years. Almost our whole education has been directed to silencing this shy, persistent, inner voice; almost all our modern philosophies have been devised to convince us that the good of man is to be found on this earth. And yet it is a remarkable thing that such philosophies of Progress or Creative Evolution themselves bear reluctant witness to the truth that our real goal is elsewhere. When they want to convince you that earth is your home, notice how they set about it. They begin by trying to persuade you that earth can be made into heaven, thus giving a sop to your sense of exile in earth as it is. Next, they tell you that this fortunate event is still a good way off in the future, thus giving a sop to your knowledge that the fatherland is not here and now. Finally, lest your longing for the transtemporal should awake and spoil the whole affair, they use any rhetoric that comes to hand to keep out of your mind the recollection that even if all the happiness they promised could come to man on earth, yet still each generation would lose it by death, including the last generation of all, and the whole story would be nothing, not even a story, for ever and ever. Hence all the nonsense that Mr. Shaw puts into the final speech of Lilith, and Bergson's remark that the *élan vital* is capable of surmounting all obstacles, perhaps even death—as if we could believe that any social or biological development on this planet will delay the senility of the sun or reverse the second law of thermodynamics.

Do what they will, then, we remain conscious of a desire which no natural happiness will satisfy. But is there any reason to suppose that reality offers any satisfaction to it? "Nor does the being hungry prove that we have bread." But I think it may be urged that this misses the point. A man's physical hunger does not prove that that man will get any bread; he may die of starvation on a raft in the Atlantic. But surely a man's hunger does prove that he comes of a race which repairs its body by eating and inhabits a world where eatable substances exist. In the same way, though I do not believe (I wish I did) that my desire for Paradise proves that I shall enjoy it, I think it a pretty good indication that such a thing exists and that some men will. A man may love a woman and not win her; but it would be very odd if the phenomenon called "falling in love" occurred in a sexless world.

Here, then, is the desire, still wandering and uncertain of its object and still largely unable to see that object in the direction where it really lies. Our sacred books give us some account of the object. It is, of course, a symbolical account. Heaven is, by definition, outside our experience, but all intelligible descriptions must be of things within our experience. The scriptural picture of heaven is therefore just as symbolical as the picture which our desire, unaided, invents for itself; heaven is not really full of jewellery any more than it is really the beauty of Nature, or a fine piece of music. The difference is that the scriptural imagery has authority. It comes to us from writers who were closer to God than we, and it has stood the test of Christian experience down the centuries. The natural appeal of this authoritative imagery is to me, at first, very small. At first sight it chills, rather than awakes, my desire. And that is just what I ought to expect. If Christianity could tell me no more of the far-off land than my own temperament led me to surmise already, then Christianity would be no higher than myself. If it has more to give me, I must expect it to be less immediately attractive than "my own stuff". Sophocles at first seems dull and cold to the boy who has only reached Shelley. If our religion is something objective, then we must never avert our eyes from those elements in it which seem puzzling or repellent; for it will be precisely the puzzling or the repellent which conceals what we do not yet know and need to know.

The promises of Scripture may very roughly be reduced to five heads. It is promised, firstly, that we shall be with Christ; secondly, that we shall be like Him; thirdly, with an enormous wealth of imagery, that we shall have "glory"; fourthly, that we shall, in some sense, be fed or feasted or entertained; and, finally, that we shall have some sort of official position in the universe—ruling cities, judging angels, being pillars of God's temple. The first question I ask about these promises is: "Why any of them except the first?" Can anything be added to the conception of being with Christ? For it must be true, as an old writer says, that he who has God and everything else has no more than he who has God only. I think the answer turns again on the nature of symbols. For though it may escape our notice at first glance, yet it is true that any conception of being with Christ which most of us can now form will be not very much less symbolical than the other promises; for it will smuggle in ideas of proximity in space and loving conversation as we now understand conversation, and it will probably concentrate on the humanity of Christ to the exclusion of His deity. And, in fact, we find that those Christians who attend solely to this first promise always do fill it up with very earthly imagery indeed— in fact, with hymeneal or erotic imagery. I am not for a moment condemning such imagery. I heartily wish I could enter into it more deeply than I do, and pray that I yet shall. But my point is that this also is only a symbol, like the reality in some respects, but unlike it in others, and therefore needs correction from the different symbols in the other promises. The variation of the promises does not mean that anything other than God will be our ultimate bliss; but because God is more than a Person, and lest we should imagine the joy of His presence too exclusively in terms of our present poor experience of personal love, with all its narrowness and strain and monotony, a dozen changing images correcting and relieving each other, are supplied.

I turn next to the idea of glory. There is no getting away from the fact that this idea is very prominent in the New Testament and in early Christian writings. Salvation is constantly associated with palms, crowns, white robes, thrones, and splendour like the sun and stars. All this makes no immediate appeal to me at all, and in that respect I fancy I am a typical modern. Glory suggests two ideas to me, of which one seems wicked and the other ridiculous. Either glory means to me fame, or it means luminosity. As for the first, since to be famous means to be better known than other people, the desire for fame appears to me as a competitive passion and therefore of hell rather than heaven. As for the second, who wishes to become a kind of living electric light bulb?

When I began to look into this matter I was shocked to find such different Christians as Milton, Johnson and Thomas Aquinas taking heavenly glory quite frankly in the sense of fame or good report. But not fame conferred by our fellow creatures—fame with God, approval or (I might say) "appreciation" by God. And then, when I had thought it over, I saw that this view was scriptural; nothing can eliminate from the parable the divine *accolade*, "Well done, thou good and faithful servant". With that, a good deal of what I had been thinking all my life fell down like a house of cards. I suddenly remembered that no one can enter heaven except as a child; and nothing is so obvious in a child—not in a conceited child, but in a good child—as its great and undisguised pleasure in being praised. Not only in a child, either, but even in a dog or a horse. Apparently what I had mistaken for humility had, all these years, prevented me from understanding what is in fact the humblest, the most childlike, the most creaturely of pleasures—nay, the specific pleasure of the inferior: the pleasure of a beast before men, a child before its father, a pupil before his teacher, a creature before its Creator. I am not forgetting how horribly this most innocent desire is parodied in our human ambitions, or how very quickly, in my own experience, the lawful pleasure of praise from those whom it was my duty to please turns into the deadly poison of self-admiration. But I thought I could detect a moment—a very, very short moment—before this happened, during which the satisfaction of having pleased those whom I rightly loved and rightly feared was pure. And that is enough to raise our thoughts to what may happen when the redeemed soul, beyond all hope and nearly beyond belief, learns at last that she has pleased Him whom she was created to please. There will be no room for vanity then. She will be free from the miserable illusion that it is her doing. With no taint of what we should now call self-approval she will most innocently rejoice in the thing that God has made her to be, and the moment which heals her old inferiority complex for ever will also drown her pride deeper than Prospero's book. Perfect humility dispenses with modesty. If God is satisfied with the work, the work may be satisfied with itself; "it is not for her to bandy compliments with her Sovereign". I can imagine someone saying that he dislikes my idea of heaven as a place where we are patted on the back. But proud misunderstanding is behind that dislike. In the end that Face which is the delight or the terror of the universe must be turned upon each of us either with one expression or with the other, either conferring glory inexpressible or inflicting shame that can never be cured or disguised. I read in a periodical the other day that the fundamental thing is how we think of God. By God Himself, it is not! How God thinks of us is not only more important, but infinitely more important. Indeed, how we think of Him is of no importance except in so far as it is related to how He thinks of us. It is written that we shall "stand before" Him, shall appear, shall be inspected. The promise of glory is the promise, almost incredible and only possible by the work of Christ, that some of us, that any of us who really chooses, shall actually survive that examination, shall find approval, shall please God. To please God . . . to be a real ingredient in the divine happiness ... to be loved by God, not merely pitied, but delighted in as an artist delights in his work or a father in a son—it seems impossible, a weight or burden of glory which our thoughts can hardly sustain. But so it is.

And now notice what is happening. If I had rejected the authoritative and scriptural image of glory and stuck obstinately to the vague desire which was, at the outset, my only pointer to heaven, I could have seen no connection at all between that desire and the Christian promise. But now, having followed up what seemed puzzling and repellent in the sacred books, I find, to my great surprise, looking back, that the connection is perfectly clear. Glory, as Christianity teaches me to hope for it, turns out to satisfy my original desire and indeed to reveal an element in that desire which I had not noticed. By ceasing for a moment to consider my own wants I have begun to learn better what I really wanted. When I attempted, a few minutes ago, to describe our spiritual longings, I was omitting one of their most curious characteristics. We usually notice it just as the moment of vision dies away, as the music ends or as the landscape loses the celestial light. What we feel then has been well described by Keats as "the journey homeward to habitual self". You know what I mean. For a few minutes we have had the illusion of belonging to that world. Now we wake to find that it is no such thing. We have been mere spectators. Beauty has smiled, but not to welcome us; her face was turned in our direction, but not to see us. We have not been accepted, welcomed, or taken into the dance. We may go when we please, we may stay if we can: "Nobody marks us." A scientist may reply that since most of the things we call beautiful are inanimate, it is not very surprising that they take no notice of us. That, of course, is true. It is not the physical objects that I am speaking of, but that indescribable something of which they become for a moment the messengers. And part of the bitterness which mixes with the sweetness of that message is due to the fact that it so seldom seems to be a message intended for us, but rather something we have overheard. By bitterness I mean pain, not resentment. We should hardly dare to ask that any notice be taken of ourselves. But we pine. The sense that in this universe we are treated as strangers, the longing to be acknowledged, to meet with some response, to bridge some chasm that yawns between us and reality, is part of our inconsolable secret. And surely, from this point of view, the promise of glory, in the sense described, becomes highly relevant to our deep desire. For glory means good report with God, acceptance by God, response, acknowledgement, and welcome into the heart of things. The door on which we have been knocking all our lives will open at last.

Perhaps it seems rather crude to describe glory as the fact of being "noticed" by God. But this is almost the language of the New Testament. St. Paul promises to those who love God not, as we should expect, that they will know Him, but that they will be known by Him (1 Cor. viii. 3). It is a strange promise. Does not God know all things at all times? But it is dreadfully re-echoed in another passage of the New Testament. There we are warned that it may happen to anyone of us to appear at last before the face of God and hear only the appalling words: "I never knew you. Depart from Me." In some sense, as dark to the intellect as it is unendurable to the feelings, we can be both banished from the presence of Him who is present everywhere and erased from the knowledge of Him who knows all. We can be left utterly and absolutely *outside*—repelled, exiled, estranged, finally and unspeakably ignored. On the other hand, we can be called in, welcomed, received, acknowledged. We walk every day on the razor edge between these two incredible possibilities. Apparently, then, our lifelong nostalgia, our longing to be reunited with something in the universe from which we now feel cut off, to be on the inside of some door which we have always seen from the outside, is no mere neurotic fancy, but the truest index of our real situation. And to be at last summoned inside would be both glory and honour beyond all our merits and also the healing of that old ache.

And this brings me to the other sense of glory—glory as brightness, splendour, luminosity. We are to shine as the sun, we are to be given the Morning Star. I think I begin to see what it means. In one way, of course, God has given us the Morning Star already: you can go and enjoy the gift on many fine mornings if you get up early enough. What more, you may ask, do we want? Ah, but we want so much more—something the books on aesthetics take little notice of. But the poets and the mythologies know all about it. We do not want merely to *see* beauty, though, God knows, even that is bounty enough. We want something else which can hardly be put into words—to be united with the beauty we see, to pass into it, to receive it into ourselves, to bathe in it, to become part of it. That is why we have peopled air and earth and water with gods and goddesses and nymphs and elves—that, though we cannot, yet these projections can enjoy in themselves that beauty, grace, and power of which Nature is the image. That is why the poets tell us such lovely falsehoods. They talk as if the west wind could really sweep into a human soul; but it can't. They tell us that "beauty born of murmuring sound" will pass into a human face; but it won't. Or not yet. For if we take the imagery of Scripture seriously, if we believe that God will one day *give* us the Morning Star and cause us to *put on* the splendour of the sun, then we may surmise that both the ancient myths and the modern poetry, so false as history, may be very near the truth as prophecy. At present we are on the outside of the world, the wrong side of the door. We discern the freshness and purity of morning, but they do not make us fresh and pure. We cannot mingle with the splendours we see. But all the leaves of the New Testament are rustling with the rumour that it will not always be so. Some day, God willing, we shall get *in*. When human souls have become as perfect in voluntary obedience as the inanimate creation is in its lifeless obedience, then they will put on its glory, or rather that greater glory of which Nature is only the first sketch. For you must not think that I am putting forward any heathen fancy of being absorbed into Nature. Nature is mortal; we shall outlive her. When all the suns and nebulae have passed away, each one of you will still be alive. Nature is only the image, the symbol; but it is the symbol Scripture invites me to use. We are summoned to pass in through Nature, beyond her, into that splendour which she fitfully reflects.

And in there, in beyond Nature, we shall eat of the tree of life. At present, if we are reborn in Christ, the spirit in us lives directly on God; but the mind, and still more the body, receives life from Him at a thousand removes—through our ancestors, through our food, through the elements. The faint, far-off results of those energies which God's creative rapture implanted in matter when He made the worlds are what we now call physical pleasures; and even thus filtered, they are too much for our present management. What would it be to taste at the fountain-head that stream of which even these lower reaches prove so intoxicating? Yet that, I believe, is what lies before us. The whole man is to drink joy from the fountain of joy. As St. Augustine said, the rapture of the saved soul will "flow over" into the glorified body. In the light of our present specialised and depraved appetites we cannot imagine this *torrens voluptatis*, and I warn everyone most seriously not to try. But it must be mentioned, to drive out thoughts even more misleading—thoughts that what is saved is a mere ghost, or that the risen body lives in numb insensibility. The body was made for the Lord, and these dismal fancies are wide of the mark.

Meanwhile the cross comes before the crown and tomorrow is

a Monday morning. A cleft has opened in the pitiless walls of the world, and we are invited to follow our great Captain inside. The following Him is, of course, the essential point. That being so, it may be asked what practical use there is in the speculations which I have been indulging. I can think of at least one such use. It may be possible for each to think too much of his own potential glory hereafter; it is hardly possible for him to think too often or too deeply about that of his neighbour. The load, or weight, or burden of my neighbour's glory should be laid daily on my back, a load so heavy that only humility can carry it, and the backs of the proud will be broken. It is a serious thing to live in a society of possible gods and goddesses, to remember that the dullest and most uninteresting person you can talk to may one day be a creature which, if you saw it now, you would be strongly tempted to worship, or else a horror and a corruption such as you now meet, if at all, only in a nightmare. All day long we are, in some degree, helping each other to one or other of these destinations. It is in the light of these overwhelming possibilities, it is with the awe and the circumspection proper to them, that we should conduct all our dealings with one another, all friendships, all loves, all play, all politics. There are no *ordinary* people. You have never talked to a mere mortal. Nations, cultures, arts, civilisations—these are mortal, and their life is to ours as the life of a gnat. But it is immortals whom we joke with, work with, marry, snub, and exploit—immortal horrors or everlasting splendours. This does not mean that we are to be perpetually solemn. We must play. But our merriment must be of that kind (and it is, in fact, the merriest kind) which exists between people who have, from the outset, taken each other seriously—no flippancy, no superiority, no presumption. And our charity must be a real and costly love, with deep feeling for the sins in spite of which we love the sinner—no mere tolerance, or indulgence which parodies love as flippancy parodies merriment. Next to the Blessed Sacrament itself, your neighbour is the holiest object presented to your senses. If he is your Christian neighbour he is holy in almost the same way, for in him also Christ *vere latitat*—the glorifier and the glorified, Glory Himself, is truly hidden.

A Sermon at the Church of St. Mary the Virgin, Oxford